Weaving, Spinning, and Dyeing

Virginia G. Hower is a self-taught weaver and former free-lance designer, advertiser, and illustrator. Her work and commissioned designs are displayed and sold in craft shops.

THE
CREATIVE
HANDCRAFTS
SERIES

VIRGINIA G. HOWER

Weaving, Spinning, and Dyeing

A Beginner's Manual

With drawings by the author

A SPECTRUM BOOK

PRENTICE-HALL, INC., ENGLEWOOD CLIFFS, NEW JERSEY

Library of Congress Cataloging in Publication Data

HOWER, VIRGINIA G.
    Weaving, spinning, and dyeing.

    (The Creative handcrafts series) (A Spectrum Book)
    Bibliography: p.
    Includes index.
        1.-Hand weaving.   2.-Hand spinning.   3.-Dyes
and dyeing—Textile fibers.   I.-Title.
TT848.H67   746.1   75-33120
ISBN 0-13-947812-4
ISBN 0-13-947804-3 pbk.

Photographs by P. Lynn Hower
Photograph on page 144 by Chris Alderman
Weavings shown on pages 16, 150, and 151 by Muriel Hart
Weaving on page 146 by Ann Packard
Cover photograph by P. Lynn Hower

A SPECTRUM BOOK

10   9   8   7   6   5   4   3   2

Printed in the United States of America

Prentice-Hall International, Inc. (*London*)
Prentice-Hall of Australia Pty., Ltd. (*Sydney*)
Prentice-Hall of Canada, Ltd. (*Toronto*)
Prentice-Hall of India Private Limited (*New Delhi*)
Prentice-Hall of Japan, Inc. (*Tokyo*)
Prentice-Hall of Southeast Asia (Pte.) Ltd. (*Singapore*)

For my mother, with gratitude

Contents

Preface   xiii

1 Weaving, an Overview   1

2 Fibers   7

    YARNS IN WEAVING, 8
    YARN STRUCTURE, 8
    YARN NUMBERING, 10
    NATURAL FIBERS, 11
    SYNTHETICS, 17
    EXPERIENCING WEAVING MATERIALS, 17

ix

3 Spinning   19

WHY SPIN TODAY? 21
VEGETABLE FIBERS IN SPINNING, 21
ANIMAL FIBERS IN SPINNING, 22
WOOL, 23
SORTING THE FLEECE, 24
COMBING WOOL, 26
TEASING WOOL, 27
CARDING WOOL, 28
LEARNING TO CARD, 29
THE SPINDLE, 34
PLYING YARNS, 44
THE SPINNING WHEEL, 46
SKEINING, 55
SCOURING, 57

4 Dyeing   59

SOME GENERAL RULES FOR HOME DYEING, 61
EQUIPMENT FOR DYEING, 61
CHEMICAL DYEING, 62
NATURAL DYEING, 62

5 Learning on the Frame Loom   71

A CONVENIENT FIRST LOOM, 72
BUYING FRAME LOOMS, 74
A FRAME LOOM TO MAKE YOURSELF, 74
PROJECT 1—STRIPED HANDBAG, 75
PROJECT 2—WALL HANGING, 87
SOME OTHER IDEAS FOR WEAVING ON A FRAME LOOM, 90

6 Recipes for Weaving   91

WRITING A DRAFT FOR A TABBY WEAVE, 91
WRITING A DRAFT FOR A TWILL WEAVE, 97
SOME OTHER WEAVES, 98

7 The Four-Harness Loom   107

TYPES OF FOUR-HARNESS LOOMS, 107
PARTS OF THE LOOM, 109
GETTING READY TO WEAVE, 110
PROJECT 3—PLACE MATS, 132
PROJECT 4—WALL HANGING, 134

PROJECT 5—ONE SCARF, 142
PROJECT 6—BABY BLANKET OR THROW BLANKET, 143
PROJECT 7—TABLE RUNNER, 145
PROJECT 8—WALL HANGING, 149

8 To Market, To Market!   153

ADVANTAGES OF SELLING HANDCRAFTS, 153
DISADVANTAGES OF SELLING HANDCRAFTS, 154
PLANNING YOUR SELLING, 155

9 Sources   159

YARNS, FIBERS, FLEECES, SPINNING WHEELS AND SUPPLIES,
LOOMS AND WEAVING SUPPLIES, AND DYEING SUPPLIES, 159
YARNS AND FIBERS, 160
LOOMS AND WEAVING SUPPLIES, 160
BOOKS, 161
CATALOG OF BOOKS, 161
MAGAZINES, 161

Index   165

Preface

Weaving, once a common household task, has come back into our lives as a popular creative art. There is something very exciting about the processes which go into making beautiful handwoven cloth. And you can't go very far in weaving without becoming curious about the spinning and dyeing of raw fibers to use on your loom. In this book you will learn to spin woolen yarn right from a fleece—both on a spindle and on a spinning wheel; you will become familiar with both chemical and natural dyes to beautify your handspun yarn; you will learn to set up and weave on a four-harness floor loom.

Many people think that weaving, spinning, and dyeing are complicated and difficult. Actually each process consists of a series of very simple steps. This book will teach you each of these steps through the use of direct language and plentiful, explicit line drawings and photographs. You will be shown everything you need to know to spin, dye, and weave. I have also included a discussion of various fibers, thoughts on selling your products, and a section on sources of tools and materials. The tone of the book is casual: technical know-how is fine in weaving, but it's more important to enjoy yourself!

Acknowledgments

I would like to thank some of the wonderful people who made it possible for me to write this book: all of my family, especially Larry, Wendy, Nicky, and Lynn for their patience and moral support; P. Lynn Hower for her excellent photographs; Muriel Hart and Ann Packard for the loan of their weavings; Chris and Derek for a fine picture; Margaret Harrison, Susan, and Janet for reviewing; and Carol of the Wilderness Road Weavers, who, long ago, sent me some of her handspun, vegetable-dyed yarns with the words, "Weave joy into your life with this."

Weaving,
Spinning, and
Dyeing

1 Weaving, an Overview

Long ago, before people ever thought of settling down and raising livestock and crops, weaving was part of their nomadic way of life. Early men and their families needed carrying mats and baskets, floor coverings, and easily erected shelters. They made all of these by interlacing long reeds and sticks. We don't know how long it took for this first weaving to evolve. No one can guess how many eons elapsed between the time when someone first noticed the weaving in nature—the bird's nest and the beaver's dam—and the moment when a human first used this knowledge in making functional woven articles. And since that time, weaving and all the other processes in the making of textiles have been of great importance in the daily lives of all peoples. For the making not only of useful but also of beautiful fabrics, weaving eventually became a highly developed art form. Over the centuries, the oringinal crude and primitive tools gave way to sophisticated weaving machines; but today weaving is essentially the same as it has always been: the interlacing of one set of fibers with another. The lengthwise fibers are called the *warp;* the fibers that interlace the warp are called the *woof* or *weft;* the woven fabric is called the *web*.

The first weavers, using rigid fibers that grew around them, made their mats and baskets with no other tools but their fingers. But when softer,

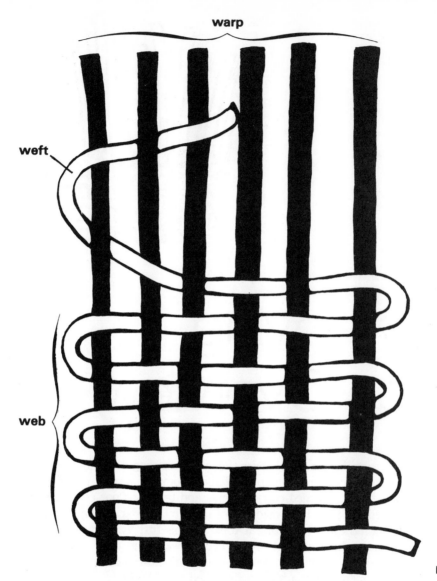

Figure 1.1

more pliable fibers such as animal hair came into use, a tool was needed to keep the lengthwise warp taut in order to facilitate the interlacing of the weft. The first *loom*, built to accomplish this stretching of the warp, seems to have been a *warp-weighted loom*. This primitive loom, which stood upright, had a horizontal beam from which the warp hung. Stones or other weights were attached to the ends of the warp to keep the fibers taut. Another early loom, which is still in use today, is the *backstrap loom*. The warp is attached at one end to a beam tied to a stationary object such as a tree and at the other end to a belt that passes around the body of the weaver. To keep the warp fibers taut, all the weaver has to do is lean back. To

2

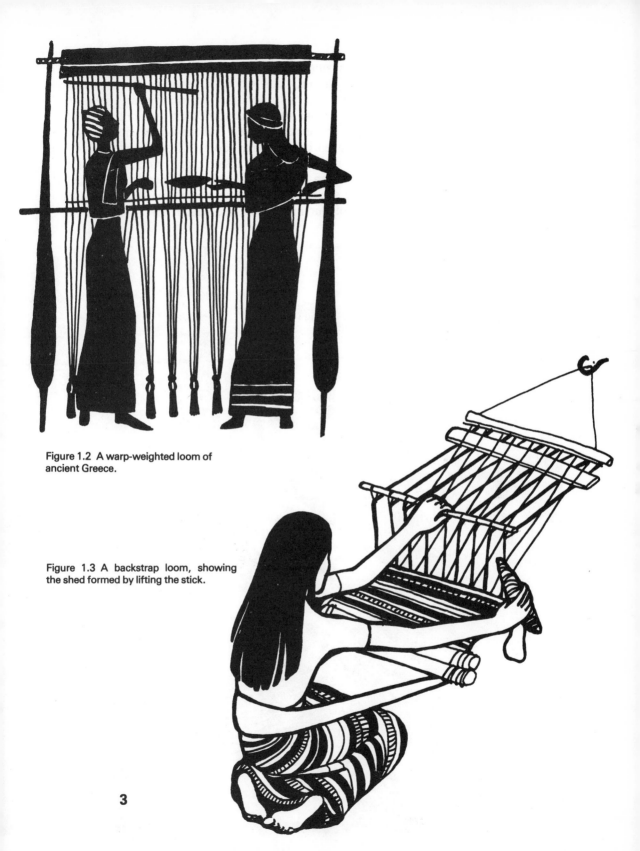

Figure 1.2 A warp-weighted loom of ancient Greece.

Figure 1.3 A backstrap loom, showing the shed formed by lifting the stick.

3

further simplify the weaving process, devices were added to the backstrap loom that lift alternate warp threads to form a space, or *shed,* for the weft to pass through. A stick with a string lifts every other warp thread in the first row, or *pick,* of weaving; a flat stick turned on its side lifts all the remaining warp threads for the second pick. Fabrics of amazing beauty and intricacy have been woven on backstrap looms. These looms are so effective that some cultures never went on to faster, more complicated looms.

The first real innovation in looms came in the Middle Ages when the Western world became aware of the Chinese looms. These horizontal looms were the forerunners of our modern looms, which have sheds formed by

pressing levers attached to *harnesses,* through which alternate warp fibers were threaded. Today's multiple-harness looms, similar in appearance to early Chinese looms, are capable of weaving fabrics of almost unlimited variety.

It wasn't too long ago that a great deal of a household's chores had to do with spinning, dyeing, and weaving all of its clothing and linens. We tend to think about all of this cozy activity with nostalgia, but it is enlightening to note how readily our forebears abandoned their spinning wheels and looms when machine made cloth became available! In colonial times it was hard work to produce the volume of fabric needed for a family's well-being.

Figure 1.4 Weaving at a four-harness floor loom.

6

Nowadays, however, when we can purchase anything we need readymade, there is a real attraction in making things ourselves, using the same tools and materials as our ancestors.

The actual physical processes of spinning and weaving are rhythmic, soothing, and enjoyable; and the thrill of creating fabric that is both functional and lovely is hard to describe. Spinning and dyeing your own yarns for knitting and weaving and weaving unusual and beautiful fabrics for your own use can be economical too. In this book you will learn how to spin wool right from a sheep's fleece, dye the handspun wool with chemical or natural colors, and weave many kinds of fabrics. Immerse yourself in this art of our ancestors, and have a good time!

2 Fibers

The first weavers of baskets and mats didn't have much choice of raw materials; they used what was available nearby. From hillsides and fields they gathered grasses and rushes, vines, willows, and twigs; they split bark and cane, peeled coconuts, cut strips of animal hide, and cleaned sinews—all to use in their sturdy, well-designed weavings. Such *nonfibrous materials* sufficed for weaving needs until clothing became necessary—or customary. Then, pliant fabrics were needed, and the cultivation of more sophisticated plant and animal *fibers* was begun for use in the preparation of flexible *yarns*.

These days we have an almost bewildering variety of materials for weaving! Not only can we still use nonfibrous materials from nature and yarns from plant and animal fibers, we can also choose from a huge range of synthetics. When you start a weaving, it is tempting to pick out any gorgeous yarn that catches your eye, but very often it turns out to be frustrating to work with or inappropriate for a particular function. A good way to avoid the pitfall of selecting the wrong yarn is to learn something **7** about different materials and their uses in weaving.

YARNS IN WEAVING

In this chapter we will glance at some of the kinds and shapes of materials available for weaving. When you visit a yarn shop or leaf through a supplier's catalog you will be very aware of the countless choices in yarns. It doesn't help much to say that as you grow in weaving expertise, you will become more efficient in picking out materials; this may be true, but when you first start to weave, how should you choose the yarn?

There are two ways: select the yarn appropriate for a specific project, or plan a project around a superb yarn! In either case, there are only a few guidelines to help you—most of your decisions will depend on your own taste and inspiration.

Some guidelines for choosing yarns are dictated by the function of the loom itself. Since a warp is stretched on a loom to provide the tension necessary for weaving, yarns to be used for warping should be *strong,* both to keep a steady tension and to withstand constant beating during weaving. Strength in yarns comes from longer fibers and extra twist in the spinning. Try to break a yarn with your fingers—if it snaps easily it won't be strong enough for the warp. Warp yarn should be *flexible* enough to reduce breakage during weaving, but not so elastic as to sag and ruin the shed. Warp yarns should also be *smooth,* to prevent catching onto each other while weaving. It takes a weaver only one experience with a mohair warp to realize how maddening a fuzzy warp can be!

Almost any yarn or nonfibrous weaving material can be used for the weft, or filling, of a woven piece—depending on the function of what you are making and also on the structure of the weave. A weft of reeds and grasses might be effective for a place mat, but it wouldn't last long in a floor rug. A wall hanging, which will seldom be washed or handled, can have such fragile weft materials as sticks, roving (combed but unspun fibers), feathers, leaves, paper, or metal strips; but a child's handwoven skirt should have a weft of some strong, washable yarn. A towel woven in a plain pattern might need the same weft as warp, while a bedspread woven in a complex pattern could require three different sizes of weft yarns. As you learn to weave, by closely examining the yarns appropriate for each project, you will learn more about the use of materials.

YARN STRUCTURE

Individual fibers come in two forms: single long stands or filaments such as in silk or rayon and short lengths as in cotton and wool. The longest fibers are the strongest, and the way individual fibers are put together determines the shape and size of the finished yarn.

Fibers which are simply bundled together and prepared for spinning are
8 fun to use in certain types of weaving. These ready-to-spin lengths of fibers,

such as wool *roving,* cotton *slivers,* and alpaca or camel *tops,* are used to add softness and bulk to wall hangings, ponchos, bags, and other thick fabric articles.

A *singles* yarn is made by twisting together or spinning many individual fibers. The thickness of a singles yarn depends upon the types of fibers used and the number of them that are twisted together. The thick-and-thin character of a singles *slub* yarn, for instance, is produced by twisting uneven amounts of fibers. The strength of singles yarns is influenced by the amount of twisting during spinning. A singles yarn with 30 twists per inch will be a great deal stronger than one (made from the same type of fiber) with 10 twists per inch.

Twisting together two or more singles yarns produces *plied* yarns (see Figure 2.1). Different colors and sizes of singles are plied together to make unusual novelty yarns. Plying increases the strength and thickness of yarns; the heaviest and most durable fabrics are often woven with plied yarns.

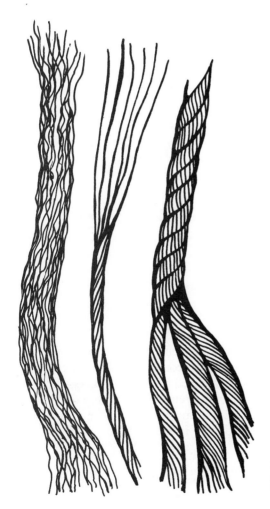

Figure 2.1 Fibers for weaving. *Left,* roving; *center,* singles yarn; *right,* plied yarn.

Figure 2.2 Some novelty yarns.

YARN NUMBERING

There is a convenient numbering system that tells us the size of yarns that we buy or order. The first number in a "yarn count" specifies the thickness of the singles yarn used to make the completed yarn. The higher the number, the finer the yarn.* The second number refers to the number of singles yarns plied together. For instance, 8/2 cotton yarn is a two-ply cotton of medium weight; while 20/1 cotton is a very fine one-ply, or singles, cotton yarn.

10   *Except in silks and most synthetics, which have a different numbering system.

NATURAL FIBERS

The scope of weaving with materials and fibers found in nature is limited only by your ingenuity. Dried weeds, pine needles, marsh grass, feathers, reeds, and leaves are all around us—ready to be woven into mats or wall hangings! Fibers from plants and animals can be machine-spun or handspun into various yarns, dyed or left natural, used in combinations or alone. They can have excellent qualities of insulation, beauty, and durability. And, it is somehow especially satisfying to work with the unique textures and colors of natural yarns. The earthy feel of homespun wool and the delicacy of pure silk thread are inspiring to any weaver.

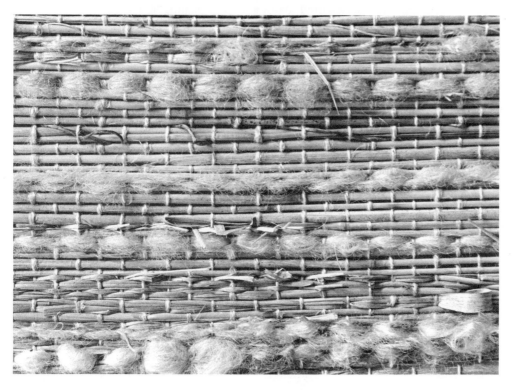

Figure 2.3 Table mat woven with reeds and roving on a synthetic warp.

PLANT FIBERS

Most of the fabric in the world is woven from *cotton,* the commonest *seed fiber.* Because fibers attached to seeds are designed to float through the air, they are strong, short, uniform, silky, and fine. Seed fibers from dandelions and milkweed pods are too sparse and short to be useful for weaving, but

11

cotton fibers conveniently grow in large, dense clumps, or "bolls," on plants that are rapidly raised in hot climates.

Cotton feels good next to the skin. It is smooth, fairly elastic, and lightweight, and has been used traditionally to weave clothing and household articles. Cotton is ideal for dyeing, and is wonderfully washable and rugged, if handled with just a little care. (Wash handwoven cotton by machine or by hand in cold water; *don't* put it in the dryer!)

Cotton is available in countless forms, from bulky "slivers" (combed ready for spinning) to the finest cotton thread. The best comes from Egypt and India, but there is a use in weaving for almost any grade. Use cotton yarns for weaving hand towels, clothes, bedspreads, tablecloths, pillow covers, place mats and napkins—anything to be used a lot and washed frequently. Weave textured bags and lace-technique hangings with cotton string, twine, and "carpet warp."

Bast fibers, which grow under the bark of all plants, are generally stiff and brittle. *Linen,* the finest bast fiber, has always been the most popular with weavers. Linen is strong and durable and becomes softer and more beautiful with age, use, and many washings. It is fairly difficult to dye, but is prized by handweavers for its smooth texture and neutral color. Linen fabric is sturdy and usually lintfree. Weave the most delicate linen thread into household linens or lacey sunlit drapes; use linen as warp in tapestries and rugs, leaving knotted fringes; weave linen upholstery fabric, tablecloths, and even linen bookcovers.

Figure 2.4 Curtain fabric woven with cotton slub yarn and raw silk stripes on a linen warp.

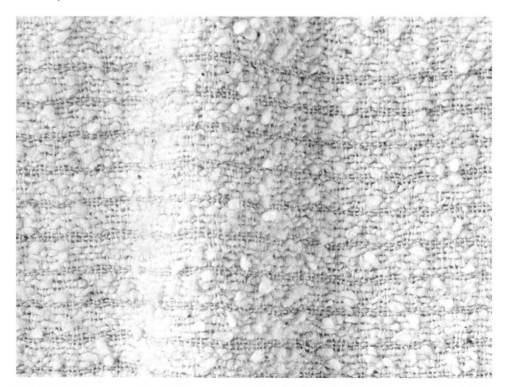

Jute and *hemp* are coarse bast fibers, made commercially into burlap, sacking, and ropes. Heavy jute yarns make excellent warp for tapestries and rugs, and are cheaper than linen. Both jute and hemp provide a splintery texture in hangings or woven sculpture and are practical for weaving certain kinds of rugs or floor mats.

ANIMAL FIBERS

Animals keep reasonably warm, dry, and insulated because they are covered with fur or hair. Long before written history, naked humans learned to protect themselves from the elements with fabric woven from animal hair. We still use yarns spun from animal fibers for weaving clothing, blankets, and many other things. Animal fur and hair can be short or long, smooth or kinky, oily or dry, soft or scratchy. There are as many natural colors of animal yarn as there are individual animals, and the fibers can be bleached and dyed with brilliant or muted colors.

Wool, the best-known animal fiber, is valuable for its beauty and practicality. The oily, wavy, elastic fibers make woolen fabric naturally resilient, water-repellent, and warm. Wool is lightweight, soft, and easy to spin (see chapter 3). There is a staggering variety of woolen yarns to use in weaving almost any kind of fabric, from the finest head scarf to the heaviest knotted

Figure 2.5 Woven goat hair.

tapestry. Wool yarn for warping should be highly twisted to strengthen the short fibers. Select the weight and shape of woolen yarn for weft filling to suit the function of the woven article. Soft, lightly twisted woolen yarn is fine for weaving a poncho, but not for sturdy rugs. Thick, irregular hand-spun wool is wonderful for very simple fabrics, such as in the handbag woven on a frame loom in chapter 5. You will soon learn to experiment with every woolen yarn you can get your hands on!

Coarser animal hair, such as goat hair and yak hair, is used for weaving such heavy and utilitarian articles as rugs and coats. You can also add interest and weight to wall hangings with these fibers; they have a scratchy texture but are often mixed with wool, alpaca or other softer fibers for use in clothing, blankets, and cushion covers.

The most luxurious animal fibers are mohair, cashmere, Angora, camel hair, llama, alpaca and vicuña. They are spun into yarns that produce fibers of unparalleled softness.

Mohair comes from the long curly fleece of Angora goats, raised primarily in Turkey. Pure mohair is horribly expensive, but blends are available which cut down weaving costs. Because mohair yarn is very fuzzy and breaks easily, it is usually unsuitable for warp. Warm, fluffy blankets can be woven with mohair filling on wool or synthetic warps. *Brushing* the fabric with a stiff hairbrush or fine carder gives it a thick, high nap. The luster and elasticity of mohair are perfect for weaving light, warm clothing. *Cashmere,* another rare goat fiber, has similar uses.

Rabbit hair, especially from the *Angora* rabbit, is soft and short, and usually combined with other fibers to spin a fluffy, slippery yarn for specialty uses. *Camel* hair has both stiff and soft fibers, and has superior insulating qualities. Spun by itself or in combination with other yarns, it is ideal for coats and blankets.

The *alpaca, llama,* and *vicuña,* are South American animals whose hairs provide fine, soft fibers. Alpaca yarn, usually a shade of brown, does not take readily to dyestuffs, and is often varied by mixing with light-colored fibers. Llama fibers are somewhat shorter and coarser than alpaca, and vicuña is longer and softer. Weavers use these expensive fibers sparingly, but they are lovely and add a superb feeling to clothes and other fabrics.

Silk is the amazing animal fiber excreted by a moth larva. The strong, hairlike silk filament unwound from one silkworm's cocoon measures up to one thousand yards! Several fibers are spun together to produce silk thread, and threads are twisted into different thicknesses of yarns. Cultivated silkworms produce fine, even fibers, while wild silkworms (fed on oak leaves) make the irregular fibers familiar in shantung silk material. The natural color of the filament is bright yellow; silk is usually bleached for dyeing. Handweaving with silk yarn is worth trying at least once! Silk has an undefinably precious feel and appearance and can add effectively to fabrics woven primarily from other fibers. Try weaving combinations of linen and silk for curtain material, or cotton and silk for an elegant shirt.

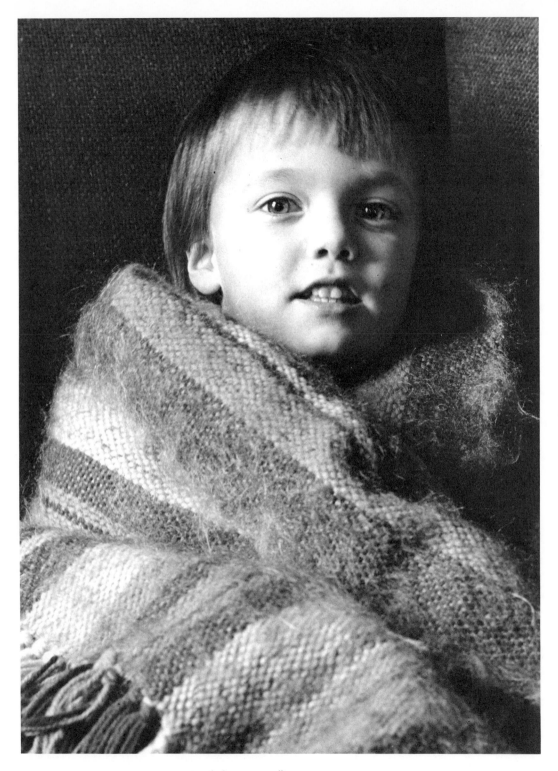

Figure 2.6 Brushed blanket woven of mohair on an acrylic warp.

Figure 2.7 Wall hanging woven with all-synthetic materials on a linen warp. (Weaving by Muriel Hart)

SYNTHETICS

The first man-made fiber, rayon, was an imitation of silk, but modern synthetics often have properties of strength and beauty not found anywhere in nature. Fibers produced from such diverse substances as wood pulp, resins, and glass are frequently more durable and versatile than natural fibers. A warp made from practically indestructible acrylic yarn is a real boon to a handweaver—there is almost no breakage of threads while weaving, and the finished web is a strong and elastic as the yarn itself. The most brilliant colors and exotic textures can be found in synthetics, and man-made novelty yarns invite experimentation in weaving. We are all aware of the benefits of easy-care synthetics for clothing, bedspreads, towels, and blankets. A woolen baby blanket is lovely but impractical; one woven from a polyester yarn is just as handsome, and can be thrown right into the dryer! Moreover, man-made fibers and yarns are much less expensive. Use them often in your weavings, and combine them with natural fibers for extra depth and beauty.

EXPERIENCING WEAVING MATERIALS

No matter how carefully a weaving project is planned, the appearance of the completed article is almost always a surprise. The proportions of color and combinations of texture in various weaves are hard to predict; it is always exciting to see the first few rows of weft as they are woven in. And even if a weaving turns out a little unexpectedly, you will probably be pleased with it—if you like the yarns to begin with.

The importance of really liking your materials can't be stressed enough. Before buying yarn, touch it, rub it, look at it in different lights, examine its construction. If the color isn't just right, or if you don't care for its feel, go on to another yarn—there are plenty to choose from. Be on the lookout for new yarn suppliers; trade yarns with other weavers; learn to spin your own! And once you have found the right yarn for a project, *enjoy* weaving with it! That's what it's all about.

3 Spinning

Long ago, sitting by a crude fire and dawdling with a bundle of cut rushes, a lake-dweller made a wonderful discovery. Drawing some rushes past others and twisting them, he found that he had made a fiber longer and stronger than a single stalk. He had spun a length of twine ideal for fishing lines or nets. *Spinning* today with a spindle or wheel is the same as it was then with fingers—it is the process of drawing short fibers past each other and twisting them to produce a continuous yarn.

From Stone Age ropemakers to American settlers in the last century, spinning was a familiar and unavoidable household task. Spinning linen from stalk fibers of flax plants and wool from sheep fleeces, women produced yarn to weave cloth for every family need. It took a great deal of time and labor to clean and prepare the fibers, spin and dye the yarn, and weave, cut, and sew the homespun fabric. No wonder the distaff and spindle came to be a symbol of womanhood!

19

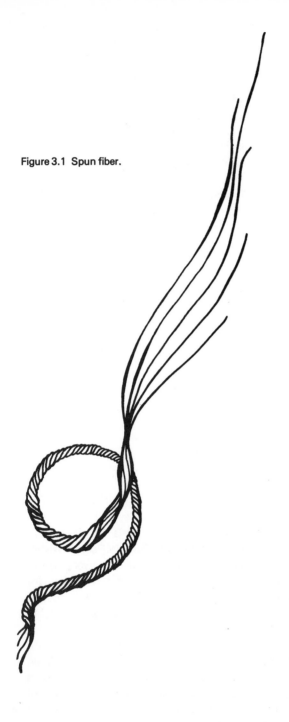

Figure 3.1 Spun fiber.

Figure 3.2 Greek woman spinning with a distaff.

WHY SPIN TODAY?

There is something quaint and cozy in the picture of a pioneer woman, sitting at her wheel by a crackling hearth, a cradle rocking gently by her side. But spinning was, for her, part of the long, often tedious process of providing cloth for household necessaries. Today we have endless varieties of machine-made yarns and fabrics for every conceivable need. Why should we bother to spin?

Spinning is a delightful pastime. The rhythm of using a spindle or wheel is soothing, and creating a length of lovely yarn from useless short fibers is a great satisfaction. It is especially exciting for a weaver to construct a fabric from his own handspun yarn. The most unique and beautiful yarns are spun by hand; unusual textures and color combinations and even the irregularities of handspun yarn cannot be reproduced in commercial yarns. And with the high cost of materials these days it makes sense to spin some of your own for weaving. Fibers for spinning usually cost less than half as much per pound as the machine-spun yarn.

It does take time to spin; the old rule-of-thumb is that it takes seven spinners to provide yarn for one weaver. Spinning all your yarn would overwhelm anyone, but handspun yarn for special projects adds a special beauty and depth to your weaving.

VEGETABLE FIBERS IN SPINNING

The earliest scraps of woven fabric, dating to the Stone Age, are made of bundles of flax fiber, twisted into threads of various thicknesses. Throughout history, from ancient Egypt to medieval times, linen thread spun from flax was used for most household weaving. The incredibly complicated process of preparing flax fibers for spinning has not changed from the earliest days. After harvest, flax plants were coarsely combed ("rippled"); the stems were fermented, dried in the sun, stripped, and cut; the fibers were cleaned ("skutched,") then pounded in a wooden trough until soft ("beetled"), after which they were combed many times ("hetchelled"). The fibers were finally wrapped around a *distaff* (usually a long stick of sorts) and spun on a spindle or wheel. The thread then had to be bleached and usually dyed before weaving the cloth. Linen is strong, durable and handsome, and can be spun to threads of unbelievable fineness. It is fairly difficult for the beginner to spin, however, as the smooth fibers tend to slide too quickly past each other. Flax prepared for spinning can be obtained through several mills and companies (see the section on yarns and fibers in chapter 9).

Other vegetable fibers that can be spun by hand are cotton, hemp, jute, sisal. Jute and sisal are coarse and splintery to spin and are usually reserved for the manufacture of ropes and twines. Hemp is not available for hand-spinning in this country.

Cotton, prepared from the pod or *boll* of the cotton plant, is difficult to handspin because of its short, smooth fibers. It is almost impossible to get good cotton for spinning unless you are lucky enough to find some Egyptian cotton. Cotton grown in the United States has the shortest fibers and is inferior for handspinning.

ANIMAL FIBERS IN SPINNING

Animal fibers most commonly used for spinning are sheep wool, goat hair (including cashmere and mohair), alpaca, human hair, yak hair, cow hair, dog hair, rabbit fur, camel hair and silk. Although all of these can be bought in this country or combed from your pets, by far the most common and versatile is sheep wool. Because wool is readily available and easy to spin, this book will deal mainly with wool spinning. The basic process of spinning, however, is similar and can be applied to all fibers.

Figure 3.3 Corriedale ewe and lamb.

WOOL

The scaly structure of wool fibers makes them cling together for ease in spinning, and their characteristic *crimp,* or waviness, gives woolen yarn and clothing superb airiness and insulating warmth. Wool grows on sheep in

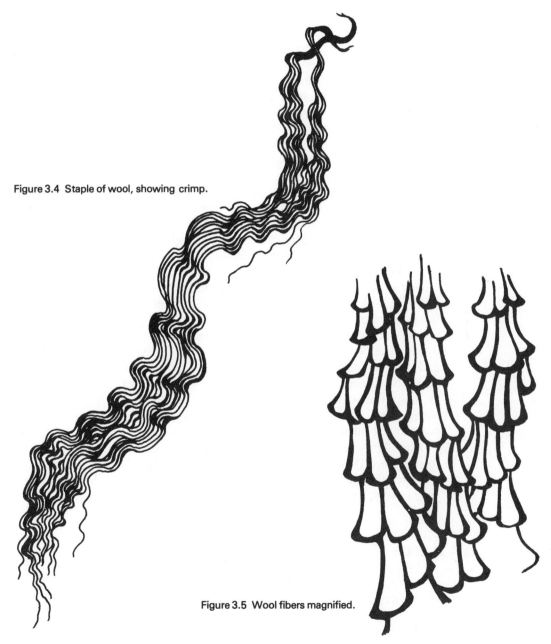

Figure 3.4 Staple of wool, showing crimp.

Figure 3.5 Wool fibers magnified.

23

clumps, or *staples,* made up of hundreds or even thousands of individual fibers. There is an oil gland at each fiber's base, which secretes *lanolin* for lubrication. The lanolin-rich oiliness of a newly shorn fleece is best for spinning, and for your hands! Olive oil must be sprinkled on old or scoured (cleaned) fleeces to soften them for spinning.

Wool comes in infinite colors and textures, depending upon the variety, breeding, age, health, and location of the sheep. The quality of sheep wool is categorized by a numbering system indicating its fineness in spinning, 100 being the best. A count of "62s to 70s" is a very fine wool breed, means that 62 to 70 yarn lengths of 560 yards each can be spun from a single pound of wool. If this confuses you, just remember that a higher count means a finer fiber. The length of the staple also varies among different breeds and individuals, from 2 inches to over 12 inches.

Merino sheep produce the finest, softest wool; but because it is short-stapled it is difficult to spin. The crossbreeds, such as Corriedale and Romeldale, have a medium-length staple of 3 to 5 inches and are excellent for beginners. Purebred medium-wool and long-wool breeds can also produce a soft, easily spun yarn. More often then not, a company won't bother to list the breed, count, or staple-length of its fleeces. Ask for a sample, then check for fineness, crimp (the more bends per inch, the softer the yarn), length (3 to 5 inches for your first attempts), and color. Every shade of brown, grey, and white can be found, and you will probably find that a true black fleece is the most expensive.

A *fleece* is the wool shorn from a sheep once or twice a year. It is first *skirted*—the worst dirt and burrs removed, then rolled into a bundle, wrapped with burlap, and tied with twine. Such a fleece will keep for years, needing no mothproofing, if it is stored in a cool, dark place. Experienced spinners like to work with a fleece in this stage ("in the grease") unless it is to be dyed before spinning. Unscoured wool is earthy, smelly, warm, and oily, and can be cleaned thoroughly after it is spun. Some prefer to use *top,* which is cleaned, combed and chemically scoured wool, and usually comes in long ready-to-spin rolls, called *roving. Lag* is a cheaper, half-combed variety, and *skirtings* are the poorest quality combings, useful only for the coarsest rug fillings.

Although wool roving is easy to buy, it is cheaper and more satisfying to prepare a fleece yourself for spinning. Not only will you have full control over the quality of the yarn, you will come to a true understanding of your raw material through the sorting, teasing, and carding processes.

SORTING A FLEECE

Sheep, like other animals, occasionally get caught in the rain or in the hot sunshine, become matted and dirty, and collect brambles and burrs while cavorting about in fields or mountains. The uneven quality of wool from different parts of the sheep are apparent in almost any fleece. Some of it, less exposed to the elements, will be long, soft and fine, with a pronounced crimp, whereas other parts may be shorter, matted, and coarse. The yarn spun from varying qualities of wool, even from the same sheep, can have significant differences in strength, softness, felting or matting tendencies, and affinity to dyestuffs. *Sorting,* or picking out similar types of wool from a fleece, is necessary if you are at all concerned about uniformity in your finished yarn.

Sorting can be a complicated and exacting process, but we will be concerned here with only the most basic division of wool types.

Figure 3.6 Sorting a fleece.

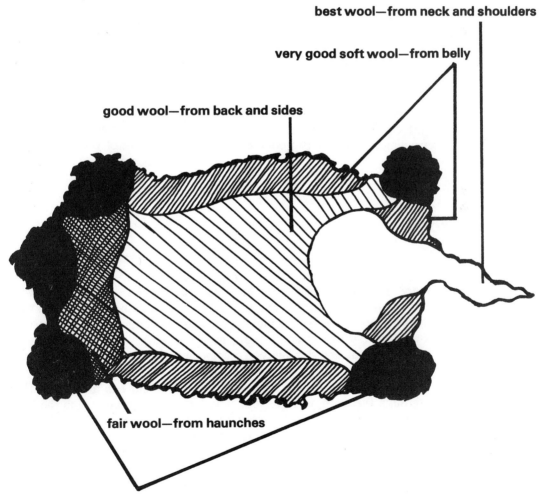

best wool—from neck and shoulders

very good soft wool—from belly

good wool—from back and sides

fair wool—from haunches

poorest wool—from tail and legs

Untie the fleece and unroll it ouside on a clear day or someplace where you have lots of room to work. You might want to spread newspapers under it, as it will probably shed burrs, dried dung, and fuzz during sorting. Look closely at the wool: some will look very soft, clean and inviting, whereas some will appear hopelessly clumped together and dirty. The poorest wool will probably be from the tail and leg regions; the best from around the sheep's shoulders and neck. Belly wool should be soft, although usually a bit crusty and matted; the sides and back should also yield good quality wool. Pull the most obviously different wool apart and divide it into piles according to length of staple, crimpiness, and softness. Don't worry about the dirt —most of it can be carded out before spinning. Or, if it is really bad, you can first *scour* it, or wash it thoroughly, following the process on page 57. After sorting the wool, divide it into paper bags or boxes, labeling them if you are especially organized. The longest stapled wool makes the strongest yarn, suitable for warp in weaving. Highly crimped wool produce wonderfully soft and airy yarn, and wool or medium length and crimp spins into a good weft yarn. As you gain experience in spinning you will know the quality of wool preferable for various types of yarn.

Now that you have sorted the fleece, there is one more step in preparing wool for spinning. The fibers are still clinging together in bunches and staples, and cannot draw past each other easily (which is, remember, the first essential part of spinning.) It is first necessary to separate the fibers and fluff them out or line them up. This is done by combing, teasing, or carding, depending on the quality wool used and the desired type of yarn.

COMBING WOOL

Combing means to separate and line up wool fibers for spinning by drawing a staple through a strong comb or carder. This method works best with a longer staple; the fibers should be at least 3 inches long. Combed wool spins into very firm, smooth yarn, good for warps and any weaving requiring strength and durability. To comb wool you will need a dog comb with steel teeth or one wool carder. Holding the comb or carder flat on a table or your lap, hold a staple of wool by the *cut end* and pull it firmly through the teeth, three or four times. Turn it over and comb the other side; then reverse the staple, holding it by the *tip end,* and repeat the process. The fibers which now lie parallel, ready to be spun, are called *tops;* the short fibers left in the comb or carder are called *noils,* which you can reserve for later carding. It takes only a few seconds to comb a staple, and you can prepare quite a few at once for uninterrupted spinning.

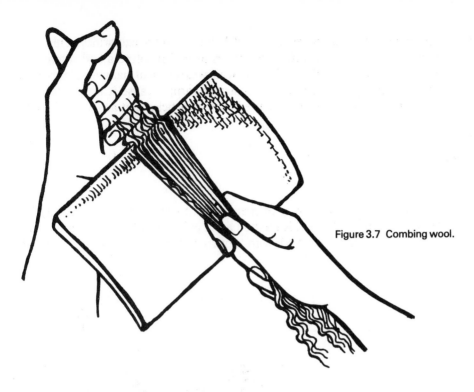

Figure 3.7 Combing wool.

TEASING WOOL

Teasing is simply pulling wool fibers apart repeatedly with your fingers until the wool is airy and cloudlike. Almost any quality of wool can be spun after just finger-teasing, except if it is very matted or has especially short fibers. Teased wool, without further carding, produces a soft, hairy yarn,

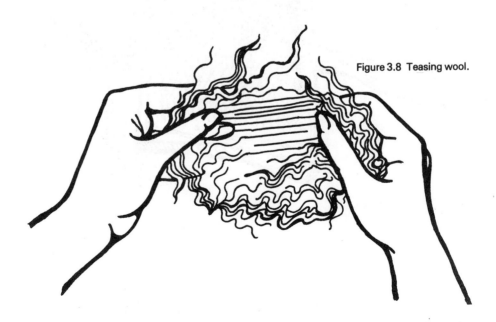

Figure 3.8 Teasing wool.

often unevenly textured because of little lumps-and irregularities. This yarn will be good for use as weft in weavings in which softness and interesting texture are needed, such as in weft-faced weaves, wall hangings, bags, and some clothing. It is not, however, a strong yarn; because it breaks easily it is not suitable for warps, heavily used rugs, or articles that are washed a lot.

CARDING WOOL

Carding is the traditional way of preparing wool for spinnin ;, especially for use as weft. The tools for this method are a pair of *carders,* which are wooden paddlelike affairs, covered with cloth or leather that has many small,

Figure 3.9 Wool carders.

bent, stiff wires attached. Carders are available at any weaving or spinning supply house, and are worth having if you plan to do much spinning. Carding raw wool produces rolls of aerated wool called *rolags,* the fibers going around the rolls in a coil-like fashion. When rolags are spun, the resulting yarn is hairy, uniform, fairly strong, and quite warm. And because you can blend different colored wool, natural or dyed, while carding, the color possibilities are endless. Carding is definitely a laborious process, but it does result in superior yarn.

LEARNING TO CARD

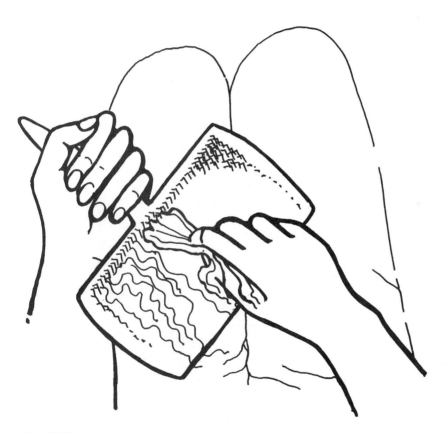

Figure 3.10

1. Place some teased wool on the left carder, which you are holding as shown and resting flat against your lap. (Fig. 3.10)

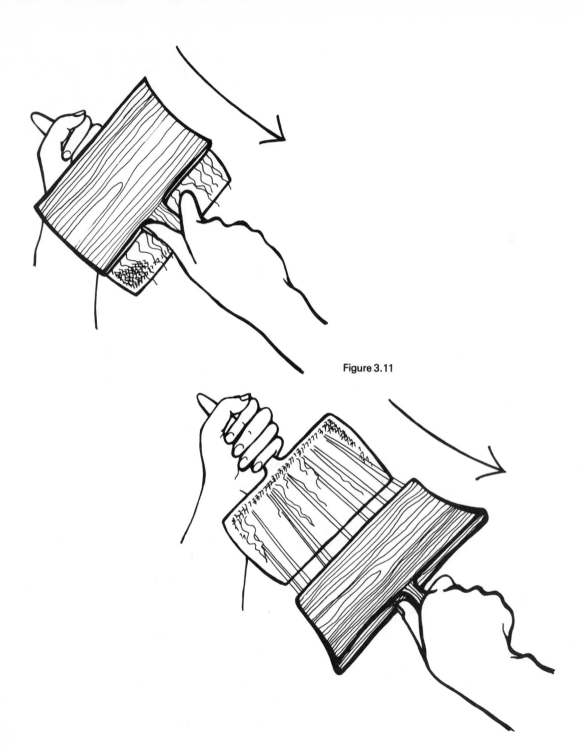

Figure 3.11

2. Draw right carder firmly across the left carder several times, until the wool starts to untangle. (Fig. 3.11)

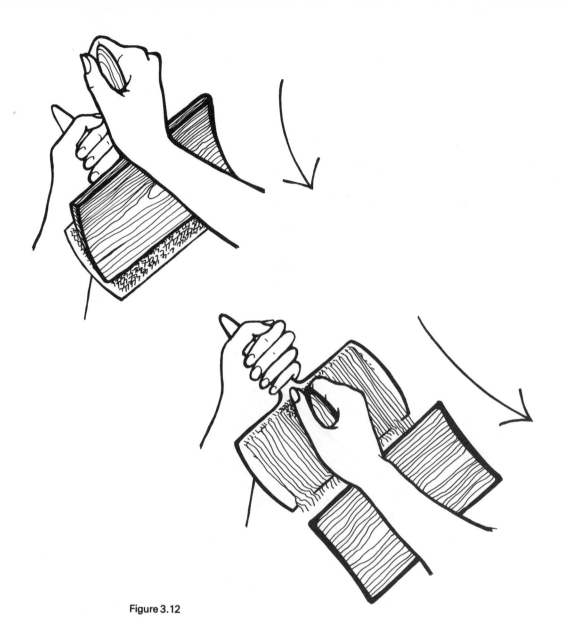

Figure 3.12

3. Turn right carder around and push it down and across the left carder; this transfers all the wool onto the left carder. (Fig. 3.12)

4. Again, with carders in original positions, draw right carder across left carder several times, as in Step 2. (Fig. 3.11)

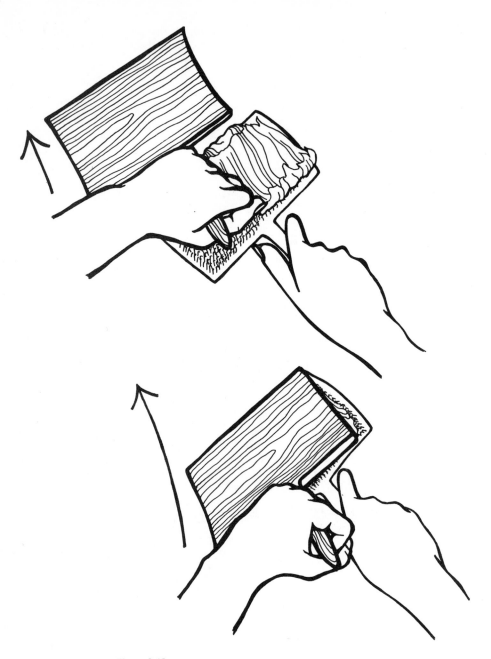

Figure 3.13

5. Turn right carder over against your lap, and draw left carder over it as shown, transferring all the wool to the right carder. (Fig. 3.13)

6. With carders in original positions, repeat the first carding process of Step 2. Keep repeating the processes in Steps 2 through 5 until the fibers are parallel and the wool is soft and uniform.

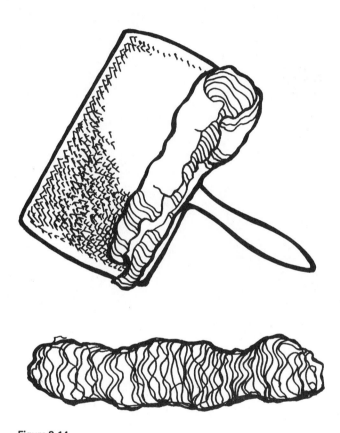

Figure 3.14

7. Transfer the wool to the left carder as in Step 3; then, *without* carding it again, transfer the wool to the right carder as in Step 5. Peel the wool, with your fingers, into a roll, or rolag, and even it out by hand-rolling it against a table or by rolling it between the backs of the carders. (Fig. 3.14)

It all seems very complicated when you are first learning to card, but after a very short while you will develop your own rhythm and be able to make perfect rolags rapidly and without even thinking about it.

Figure 3.15 *Left,* combed wool; *center,* teased wool; *right,* carded rolag.

THE SPINDLE

Nobody knows who first invented the spindle; but we do know that it was the only way of spinning until around the fifteenth century, when the spinning wheel was developed. Ancient Egyptians spindle-spun incredibly delicate linen thread to be woven into the sheerest of fabrics. References to spindles in Greek and Roman mythology and in the Bible suggest that they were very common household tools throughout history. Today, spindles are still used by scattered primitive peoples to spin coarse yarns from animal fur.

A *spindle* consists of a *shaft* or stick, notched on the top, and a removable *whorl,* or disc, near its bottom, or *nob.* The weight of the spindle pulls the fibers being spun; the whorl balances the spindle as it spins around and supports the spun yarn after it has been wound on the shaft. Spindles can **34** be home-made from sticks, knitting needles, or crochet hooks for the shaft, and half-potatoes or other weights for the whorl. However, since well-made spindles are quite inexpensive at weaving and spinning supply houses or craft shops, it makes sense to buy one. Learning to spin should always start on a spindle. Whereas spinning wheels can be confusing or intimidating to

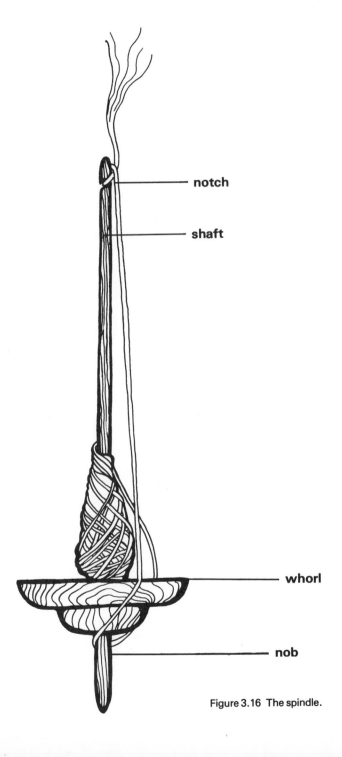

— notch

— shaft

— whorl

— nob

Figure 3.16 The spindle.

beginners, on a spindle you can really see what is happening to the fibers as they are drawn out and twisted. And spindles are not just learning devices—they are wonderfully versatile and are used by experienced spinners to make not only heavy, textured, or specialty yarns but also finer yarns of amazing softness.

SPINNING WITH A SPINDLE

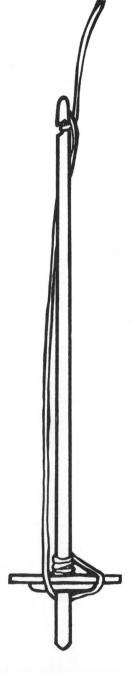

Figure 3.17

1. Tie a yard and a half or so of strong, hairy yarn to the spindle shaft, wind it around the shaft a few times, loop it around the nob, and bring it up to the top, attaching it with a half-hitch to the notch. You will be turning the spindle around in a clockwise direction, and keeping it spinning continuously by giving it occasional quick twists with your right hand. Try spinning it around now, just to get the feel of it, as you hold the yarn with your left hand. (Fig. 3.17)

Figure 3.18

2. Now, hold some teased wool in your left hand (draped over the back of your hand so it won't get tangled), overlapping the wool a few inches over the yarn. Hold the wool and yarn together with the left hand, give the spindle a clockwise spin with the right hand (Fig. 3.18), and then . . .

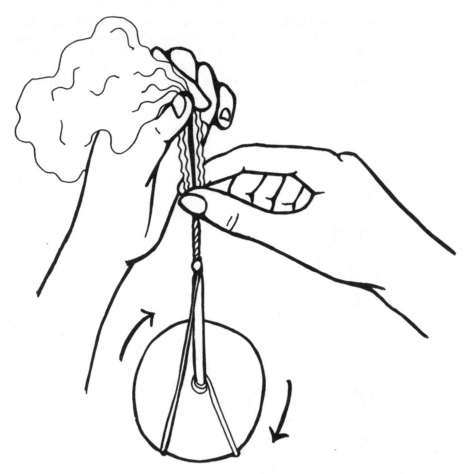

Figure 3.19

3. ... hold the yarn with the right hand also, a few inches below the left hand. (Fig. 3.19)

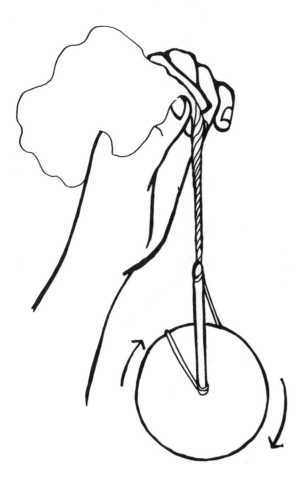

Figure 3.20

4. After the spindle has turned several times, let go with your right hand, and the fibers will twist together with the yarn. (Fig. 3.20)

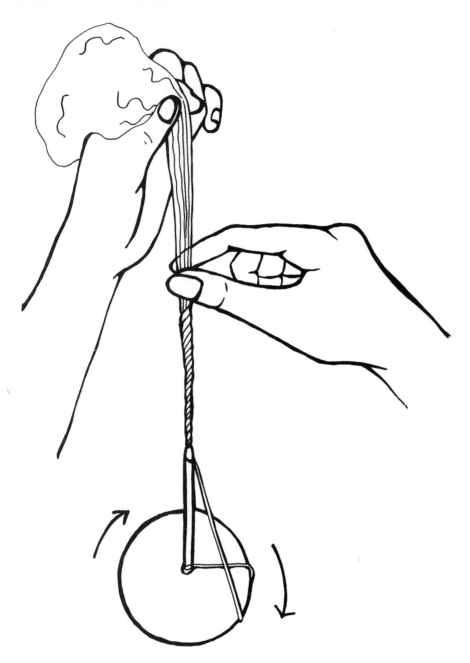

Figure 3.21

5. Give the spindle another twist, and bring the right hand back to where the left hand is holding the yarn. Move the left hand back three inches or so, pulling and drawing out the fibers of wool, and let the spindle turn around a few times. (Fig. 3.21)

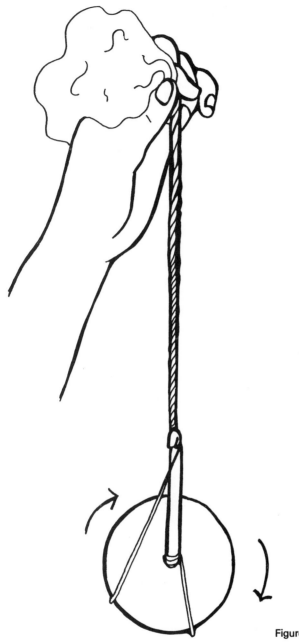

Figure 3.22

6. Let go with the right hand, and the fibers will twist as before. Keep repeating these steps to spin a continuous yarn. Don't worry right now about how it looks; if you are like most people, your yarn is breaking constantly and the spindle keeps dropping to the floor. Don't get discouraged! Just keep practicing until you have spun about a yard, no matter how gnarled it looks. If you are standing up, spin until the spindle is suspended just above the floor. (Fig. 3.22)

41

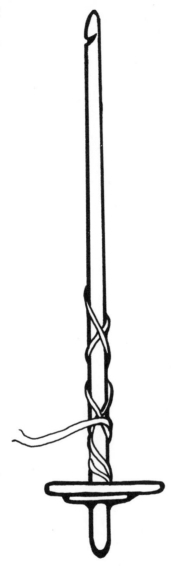

Figure 3.23

7. Undo the half-hitch and the loop around the nob, and wind the spun yarn onto the shaft as shown, leaving enough yarn free to wind around the spindle as in Step 1. (Fig. 3.23) Get ready to spin as before, repeating the whole process. When there is a good-sized cone of spun yarn on the spindle, remove it by pushing up with the removable whorl; or skein it directly from the spindle. After awhile, you will be able to skillfully pull a few fibers at a time to make a uniform yarn. The *number of fibers* drawn up in this way determines the thickness of the yarn. The *amount of twisting* in the spun yarn varies its strength and texture.

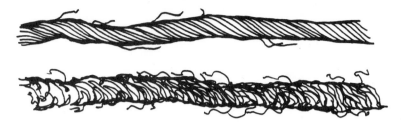

Figure 3.24 *Top,* worsted spun wool; *bottom,* woolen spun wool.

Spinning with *teased* wool, as we have just done, or with *carded rolags,* is called *woolen spinning,* producing hairy, soft yarn. Spinning with *combed* wool is known as *worsted spinning,* and gives smooth, strong yarn. The process of spinning is the same in both types; experimentation will teach you the best way of drawing out and twisting variously prepared fibers.

Figure 3.25

43

PLYING YARNS

Figure 3.26 Spun yarn with Z twist and S twist.

Turning the spindle *clockwise,* as we have just done, makes *Z-twisted* yarn. *S-twisted* yarn is spun by turning the spindle in the opposite, or *counter-clockwise,* direction.

To make *plied* yarns—two or more yarns twisted together for added strength and bulk—you will need a device called a *lazy Kate,* which holds the yarns separate and feeds them to you for twisting together with the spindle or wheel. A lazy Kate can be bought from a spinning supplier or made by fastening dowels to a board.

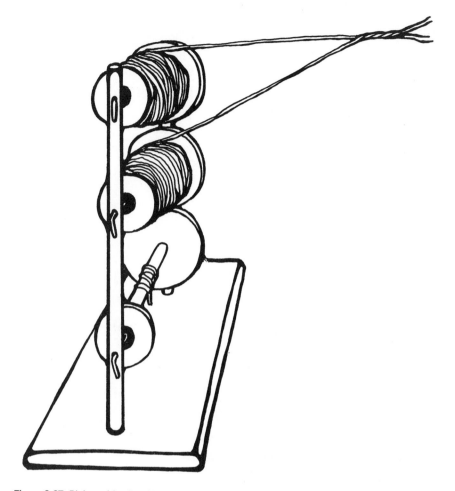

Figure 3.27 Plying with a lazy Kate.

A soft two-ply yarn is made by twisting two yarns together in the *opposite* direction from which they were spun. For instance, ply two Z-twisted yarns together by spinning them with an S twist (turning the spindle or wheel counterclockwise). Three or more yarns can be plied for added texture, strength, and bulk. A hard, sturdy plied yarn such as used by the Navahos for their blanket weaving is made by twisting yarns together in the *same* direction in which they were spun. For this type of plied yarn, ply Z-twisted yarns by spinning them with a Z twist. Unusual variegated yarns can be created by plying together yarns of different colors or thicknesses.

45

Figure 3.28 Two- and three-ply Z-twisted yarns (plied with an S twist).

THE SPINNING WHEEL

A *spinning wheel* is nothing more than a spindle turned on its side and revolved by mechancial means. The horizontal spindle is supported by two uprights, and a cord around the whorl also circles a wheel, which is turned by hand or foot power. The first spinning wheels, originating in India, were introduced to Europe in the Middle Ages. The greatly increased speed of spinning and the improved uniformity of yarn spun with wheels were probably gladly welcomed by weary medieval women, and are still much appreciated by modern spinners There are two basic types of spinning wheels: the high wheel, revolved by hand power, and the low wheel, powered by a foot treadle. Linen wheels have distaffs attached to them. High

46

Figure 3.29

Figure 3.30 High wheel.

wheels are reminiscent of early America; pioneer women walked miles every day as they stepped back and forth in front of their spinning wheels. However, as low wheels are now prevalent and can be brought in great variety, we will use them exclusively here for learning about spinning with wheels.

BUYING A WHEEL

If you have found an old spinning wheel in your grandmother's attic, leave it there—or at best use it as a planter. A spinning wheel must be well-balanced for smooth action, and old wheels usually are warped or have parts missing. New wheels can be bought ready-made and finished or unassembled and unfinished from countless suppliers. Before buying a wheel, though, it would be wise, if possible, to try out the different types. Look at the size of the orifice or eye through which the yarn will pass; to spin very bulky yarns you will need a large opening. Test different wheels for ease in treadling—some wheels will seem more comfortable to you than others. Are you concerned with a wheel's appearance? All-metal wheels are functional but not beautiful. If you have a friend who owns a spinning wheel, borrow it for a while and see how you like it before investing in one yourself.

48

SPINNING WITH A WHEEL

Spinning wool on a low wheel is actually a great deal like spinning with a spindle; the main difference is that the *twist* is caused by the foot-powered turning of the wheel, so that both hands are free to control the *drawing out* of the fibers.

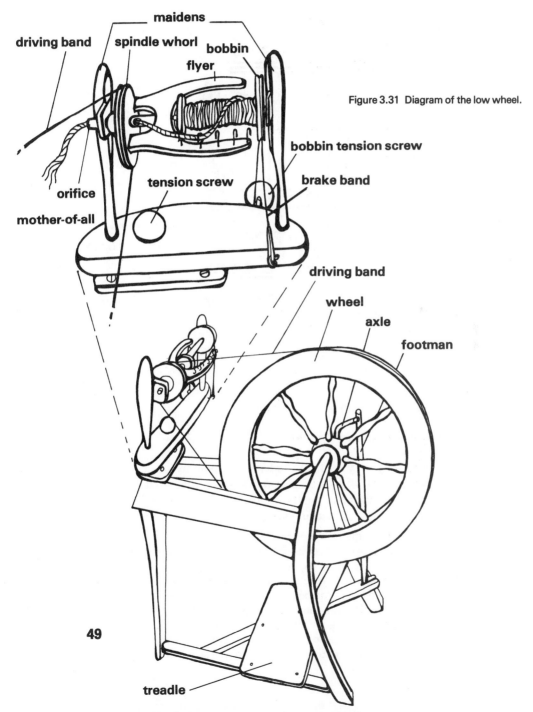

Figure 3.31 Diagram of the low wheel.

Before actually attempting to spin, learn the parts of the wheel as illustrated and figure out how they work on *your* wheel. Although there are many differences in types of spinning wheels, the working parts are generally quite similar.

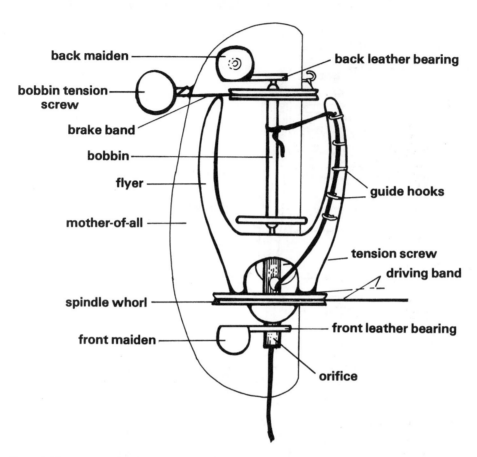

Figure 3.32 Preparing the wheel for spinning (top view).

The only way to truly understand spinning on a wheel is to try it! Sit down in front of your wheel on a stool or chair that is high enough so that your right foot rests lightly on the treadle. (You will probably prefer spinning barefoot or in stocking feet.)

1. Attach the *driving band:* Turn the *tension screw* about halfway. If you have a wheel with an adjustable *brake band,* as pictured, the driving band passes around the wheel and the spindle whorl only. The brake band will pass around the bobbin groove and be attached to the bobbin tension screw. Its purpose is to control the speed of the bobbin's turning. The bobbin must turn a bit slower than the flyer to allow the spun yarn to wind on. If your wheel has a *double driving band,* wind a strong cotton cord around the wheel, around the bobbin groove, around the wheel again, and around the back groove of the spindle whorl. Tie the ends tightly together, and turn the tension screw until the driving band is taut.

Tie a few yards of strong, hairy yarn to the bobbin, draw it along the guide hooks, and through the orifice with a crochet hook or bent wire. Turn the wheel slowly by hand and check to see that the yarn is drawn in through the orifice slowly. If not, tighten the tension screw, or, if you have one as shown, the bobbin tension screw. Generally, only a very slight tension increase is necessary. (Fig. 3.32)

2. Turn the wheel clockwise by hand, always by its spokes, not its rim. You will notice that the *treadle* moves up and down as the wheel goes around. Press down on the treadle just as it starts to go down by itself. Continue to do this until the wheel is revolving by treadle power alone. It might take a little practice, but it is important to be able to treadle without thinking about it (and without the wheel reversing its direction!) so you can pay attention to your hands. For ease in treadling, the wheel should be well-oiled often with light household oil, in every joint and turning place.

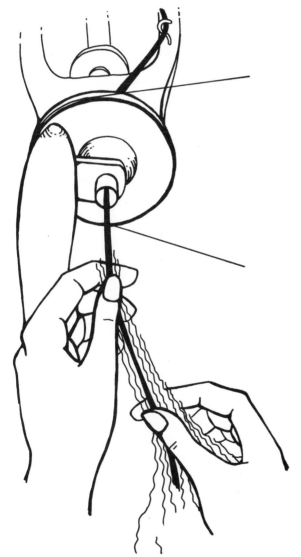

Figure 3.33

3. Take a handful of teased wool and draw out some fibers next to the yarn. Give the wheel a turn and start treadling. Hold the wool and yarn together with both hands as shown for a few turns of the wheel. (Fig. 3.33)

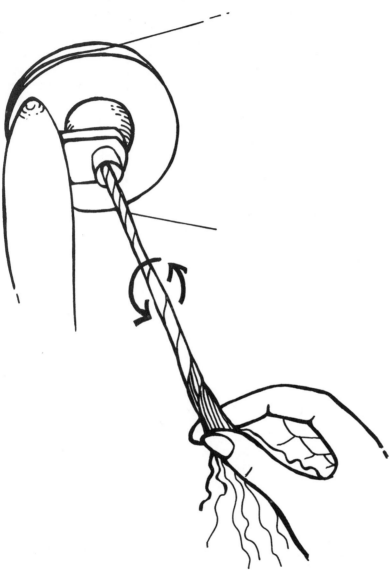

Figure 3.34

4. Then, let go with the fingers closest to the wheel. The fibers will twist together with the yarn. (Fig. 3.34)

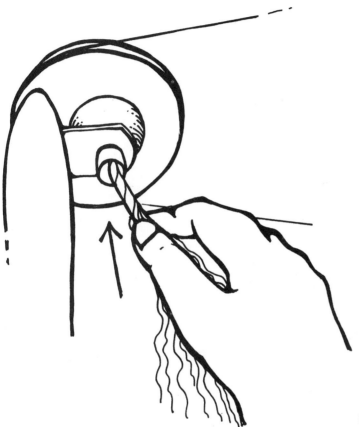

Figure 3.35

5. As the wheel continues to turn, let the newly spun yarn be drawn into the orifice, and hold the unspun fibers from being drawn in. (Fig. 3.35)

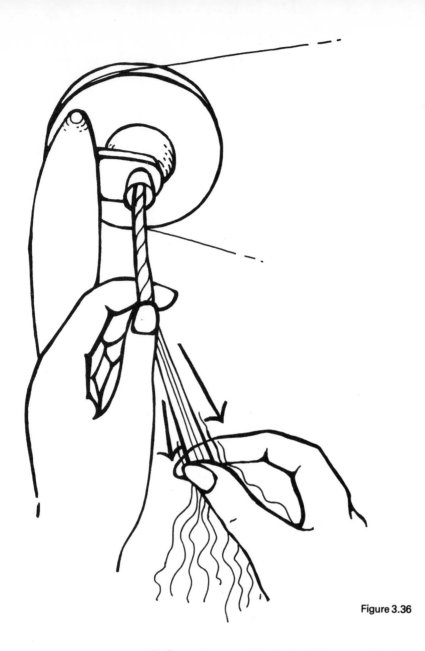

Figure 3.36

6. Grasp the yarn with the hand closest to the wheel; draw the fibers out with the further hand. (Fig. 3.36) After a few wheel revolutions, let go with the fingers closest to the wheel, as in Step 4. After the fibers become twisted, let the yarn be drawn in, as in Step 5. As you gain confidence in spinning, you will be able to increase the distance between hands while drawing out the fibers and while letting the twist run up the fibers. Don't panic if the yarn breaks or is whisked completely into the orifice. Just pull it out again with the little bent wire or crochet hook, and start over. Don't be afraid to hold onto the yarn—it will just twist a bit more. Just like learning with the spindle, beginning on the wheel may take a bit of frustration before you master it.

54

7. Adjusting the tension: the amount of twist and the speed of the drawing-in are controlled by adjusting the tension. *Less* tension gives *more* twist, as the yarn is drawn in more *slowly*. *Increased* tension makes a *less* twisted yarn, which is drawn in more *quickly*. If the yarn is being drawn in too slowly, and is overtwisted, increase the tension. If it is drawn in too quickly, causing lots of breakage or underspun yarn, loosen up the tension.

Tension can be adjusted in several ways. One method uses the *two grooves on the spindle whorl* that appear on some wheels. When the driving band is around the deeper groove, or the one nearest the bobbin, tension will be decreased, as the driving band will be less taut. To increase tension, place the driving band around the shallower, or farther, groove.

The speed of the drawing-in and the amount of twist can also be controlled by the *tension screw*. When it is tightened, it causes the driving band to become more taut, turning the flyer more quickly, and drawing the yarn more quickly into the orifice.

Another important means of controlling tension is the *bobbin tension screw* that is found on some wheels. Tightening this screw decreases the amount of twist and causes the yarn to be drawn in more quickly.

The tension can be adjusted, too, by moving the *leather bearing* on the front maiden (see diagram in Step 1). If the bearing is turned so that it presses against the spindle shaft, the amount of twist and the rate of draw will be decreased. As you constantly adjust the tension when learning to spin, you will soon grow familiar with these different methods.

As you spin, keep moving the yarn from one guide hook to the next, and then back the other way, so that the bobbin is evenly filled. Remove full bobbins to be skeined or plied with other yarn.

The *woolen method* of spinning is the same on the wheel as on the spindle: using teased wool or carded rolags. Spinning with combed wool is called, as before, the *worsted method*. Z-twisted yarn is produced by turning the wheel in a clockwise direction, and S-twisted wool by turning it counterclockwise. To ply with a wheel, follow the same procedures as with a spindle.

SKEINING

After yarn has been spun, either with a spindle or on a wheel, it should be *skeined,* or wound carefully, before being cleaned or dyed. Skeining consists of winding the yarn around a *niddy-noddy, warp reel, umbrella swift,* two pegs of a warping board, two chair backs, or two sticks in the ground. Wind it with an even tension and tie each skein *loosely* in at least four places, so it won't end up like a tangle of spaghetti during scouring or dyeing.

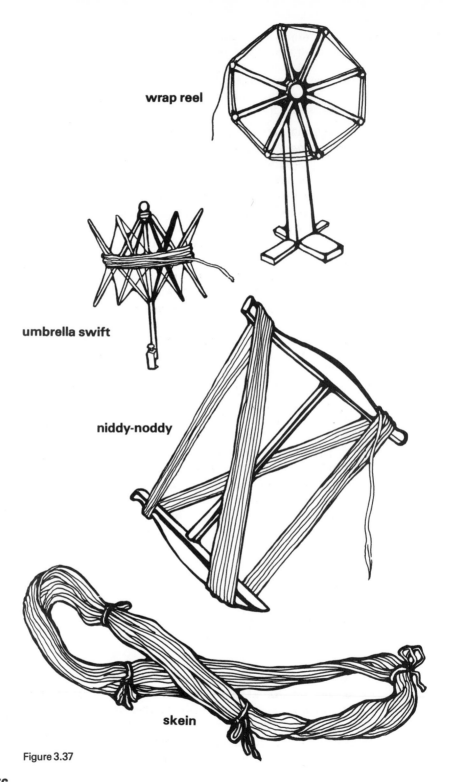

wrap reel

umbrella swift

niddy-noddy

skein

Figure 3.37

56

SCOURING

Your beautiful handspun wool can now be woven, and washed afterwards. Most spinners, however, like to wash the wool thoroughly first. And if it is to be dyed, a good *scouring* is necessary.

Make a rich, sudsy bath for your wool in very hot water with ordinary detergent or dishwashing liquid. Let it cool until you can put your hand in; then, immerse the wool. Stir it lightly around with a stick or wooden spoon and let it soak for a few minutes. Do not scrub, wring, or in any way mangle the wool—it might get hard and matted. Rinse the wool with lots of very warm water, and repeat the washing and rinsing process. Squeeze the last-rinse water very gently out of the wool. The skeins should then be hung outside in a cool, breezy place, with weights at the bottom to retain their shape. They can be strung over a clothesline and weighted with a broomstick. The wool will probably take several days to dry.

And then, there it is—the yarn that you spun yourself—from scratch! Ready to be rolled into balls for storage, wound onto bobbins or shuttles for weaving, or dunked into a dyebath, your handspun woolen yarn is unique, irreplaceable, and lovely.

Figure 3.38 Handspun skeined wool and spindle.

4 Dyeing

Dyeing is a purely decorative art. It doesn't add durability or strength to fibers—only beauty. Home dyeing is a very old occupation which hasn't lost any of its appeal for modern craftsmen. People of Peru used to wade out into the shallows and drain juices from certain mollusks to make a deep purple for dyeing. Like these ancient dyers, we find that weaving with the ivories, blacks, and browns of undyed natural yarns is not always enough; sometimes we must express ourselves with the explosive force of color.

There is a rainbow of commercially colored yarns available for weaving, but at some point you will probably want to dye your own. Perhaps you will be looking for a yarn of a *specific* color; in that case, hand dyeing with chemicals is the perfect answer. *Chemical dyeing* produces usually colorfast yarns of exact tones, for perfect matching or for carrying out a structured design. On the other hand, *natural dyes,* made from plant and animal matter, are great for color experimentation. They give yarns approximate colors, which can vary widely depending on such factors as the maturity and age of the dye plant, the season and climate of its location, and whether it is fresh or dried. Naturally dyed yarn is often less colorfast than yarn dyed with chemicals, but if it does fade, the results are wonderfully muted shades. The vast selection of dye colors, both commercial and natural, and striking variations in methods make dyeing a very creative process.

Fibers can be dyed at any stage of spinning or weaving. When *unspun fibers,* such as a fleece or roving, are dyed, they can be mixed with other colors during carding and spinning to give the impression of a third color. A blend of black and white, for instance, appears to be grey in the spun yarn, whereas a mixture of blue and yellow will seem a rich green from a distance.

You can dye a *woven fabric* after its completion, although there is always a possibility of shrinkage. Special textile-dying techniques, such as tie-dye or batik (wax-resist dyeing), are applied at this stage. But most weavers prefer to dye *yarns,* spun either by hand or commercially, to use in their projects.

Neatly tied skeins of yarn are easier to handle in a dyebath than soggy wads of fleece or roving, and yarn colors can be mixed effectively both in plying and in weaving itself. Two, three, or more entirely different colors, or shades of the same color, can be plied together. In the simplest method of mixing colors in weaving, a contrasting warp and weft can be made to look like a third color. A red weft and yellow warp, for example, will appear orange when interlaced in a simple weave. You will learn to experiment in weaving with colors. Narrow or wide stripes, checks, plaids, and diagonals can greatly alter the values and tones of the original yarns.

Top-dyeing is a way of varying yarn color by using two or more dyebaths to obtain a third color. Also, dyes will turn out differently when applied to different colors of wool. A yellow might appear clear and bright on white wool, dull and muted on grey wool.

"Dyeing" means to saturate a fiber with color. The type of fiber, its condition, and the kind of dye determine the success of the color change. Linen and cotton don't "take" dyestuffs well, whereas wool fibers and many synthetics soak up color like sponges. In this chapter we will emphasize dyeing with wool because it is the easiest fiber to handle and the most successfully dyed.

Chemical dyes and some natural dyes are effectively absorbed by fibers. They are called *substantive* dyes and need no additives to be colorfast and longlasting. Most natural dyes, however, will not adhere permanently to fibers unless they are used in combinations with solutions called *mordants.* The mordant is absorbed by the fiber, and the dye adheres to the mordant. Yarn is generally soaked in the mordant before dyeing, although there are exceptions. Different mordants can also be used to change the color of the same dyebath. For instance, wool dyed with *cochineal* (made of crushed beetles) turns red with an alum mordant and purple with a chrome mordant.

SOME GENERAL RULES FOR HOME DYEING

1. *Remember that most dyes and mordants are poisonous* to some degree. Some of them look tempting enough to sprinkle on birthday cakes, so keep them in clearly labelled jars behind lock and key, or at least out of reach of the most curious child. Do not breathe in the fumes of mordant or dye solutions; make a practice of keeping the lids on all dyepots. Don't make the mistake of using dyeing equipment for household cooking or eating. Set aside the dyepot and utensils in a special place, and scrub counters thoroughly after a day of dyeing. Dyeing is done with large quantities of very hot water. Keep the steaming pots on back burners so no one will get scalded.

2. Skein the yarn before dyeing (see page 55). Tying the skeins loosely in at least four places will keep the yarn untangled and insure even dyeing.

3. Wool (or any yarn) should be clean. Some dye books recommend soap washings or scourings, but I prefer detergent (such as dishwashing liquid) as it rinses out more easily. In any case, make sure the yarn is free from grease and dirt and is thoroughly rinsed.

4. Work with wet wool; wet the wool before mordanting, and if it is dried after mordanting, soak the skeins in clear water before dyeing. Dry yarn plunked into a mordant or dyebath results in streaking.

5. Handle wool gently to prevent matting or "felting." Stir the yarn in the mordant solution and dyebath slowly and infrequently. Don't let the temperature of the water change drastically! This can ruin the wool. Don't ever wring or twist wool; press water out gently.

6. Use soft water if possible. The minerals in hard water can cause streaky dyeing. If you can, collect rain water to use in dyeing; if not, add a little vinegar, ammonia, or commercial softener such as Calgon.

EQUIPMENT FOR DYEING

You will need at least one large pot for dyeing. The best is a huge enamel pot—the kind used for canning or for steaming lobsters. They are fairly cheap, and can also be found at junk shops or barn sales. The pot must hold four or five gallons comfortably. Stainless steel or copper pots can be used too, if you feel extravagant. Just don't use tin, iron, or aluminum utensils as they will react with the dyes or mordants.

For stirring, use wooden sticks, paddles, spoons, or glass rods. Again, stay away from metals.

Rubber gloves prevent dyed hands. It you do get some dye on your skin, most of it can be scrubbed off with Fels-Naptha or other strong hand soap.

Good measuring equipment is very helpful in dyeing. Suppliers have very precise scoops and scales to measure grams and fractions of ounces; but a baby scale or a flour scale, a quart jar, a glass measuring cup, and a tablespoon will do fine. Also, a very fine strainer or some cheesecloth is needed to strain natural dyes.

CHEMICAL DYEING

To dye with chemicals, follow the directions that come with the dye. The packets of dye obtainable at the supermarket are fine to use alone or mixed together, and exact colors can be achieved by using more precise dyes that can be ordered from special suppliers (see chapter 9).

NATURAL DYEING

MORDANTING WOOL

Most natural dyes need mordants to make the colors permanent. Early dye recipes specify such handy mordants as salt, rusty nails, and urine, but nowaday the usual solutions are made of store-bought chemicals. The most common are alum (potassium alum), chrome (potassium bichromate), iron (ferrous sulfate), copper sulfate (blue vitriol), tin (stannous chloride), household ammonia, cream of tartar, and vinegar. They are all available from suppliers (see chapter 9). We will discuss only mordanting with alum and chrome, as they are most frequently used, and are good for affixing many different dyestuffs. For recipes containing other mordants, consult one of many dye books available (see chapter 9). *All mordant and dye recipes are for one pound of wool.*

ALUM MORDANT. Dissolve ⅓ cup alum (3 ounces) and 3 tablespoons (one ounce) cream of tartar in 4 gallons of cold water (use your special dyepot). Place one pound of wool skeins (that have been wetted) in the solution, and bring the whole thing very gradually to a boil. Simmer it gently for an hour, turning the wool a couple of times, then take the pot off the burner and let it cool overnight. Squeeze most of the moisture out of the wool, and roll the skeins in a towel or put them in a plastic bag. If stored in a cool place, they will last in this moist condition for a week or so until you are ready to dye. The mordanted wool can also be used immediately, or hung out to dry and thoroughly soaked just before dyeing.

CHROME MORDANT. Chrome is extremely light-sensitive, and will give streaky dye results if not handled with care. To prevent exposure to light, keep the pot covered at all times and dye the wool *right* after mordanting. Dissolve one tablespoon (½ ounce) of chrome in ½ cup of boiling water. Add it to 4 gallons of lukewarm water and stir. Throw in the wetted wool and cover the pot. Bring to a gradual boil and simmer for an hour, turning it just a couple of times. Let it cool just until the wool can be handled. Rinse the wool in water of the same temperature as the warm mordant solution, and keep it covered until the dyebath is ready.

MAKING NATURAL DYES

Collect dye materials to use in a specific recipe, or for your own color experiments. You can always use such common household staples as coffee, tea, or onion skins. Or take a bag with you whenever you are on a picnic or hike; scrape lichens from rocks, pick bunches of ferns, crumble bark (from *dead* trees or branches), select leaves or berries and fruits from trees. Use good sense in your selections—if you are picking wildflowers for a special dye recipe, don't take every plant you see; leave some to grow back. The strongest dyes come from plants picked before maturity. A general rule is to use one peck (about one big grocery bagful) of material to make dye for one pound of wool; but if the materials are dried before dyeing, you'll need much less. Store all your bits of bark and leaves and other materials in paper bags in a dry place to prevent molding. Or you can use everything fresh. You will find that most natural dyes produce colors ranging from yellows to greens to browns and oranges. Certain colors can be obtained from natural dyes available only from a supplier because they are rare or difficult to prepare.

Pure colorfast reds, for instance, must be produced by using *cochineal* or *madder.* The best natural blues come from *indigo,* which must be used in a rather complicated method of dyeing.

The usual method of making dye is to cover the plant material with water, boil it for a little while, strain it, and add more water, enough to make 4 gallons. Once you get the hang of dyeing, you'll be searching out old and new recipes in dye books, and making all kinds of experiments on your own. It is a good idea to keep a notebook to record all dyeing attempts, including samples of the wool before and after dyeing. Also make a note of when and where you obtained the dye materials, the quantities used, the time it was boiled, and so on. It sounds like a lot of trouble, but it can help you to avoid making mistakes twice. And if you come up with a superb color, you might want to know how to get a similar result in the future.

Here are some easy recipes to get you started on what might be a real adventure in dyeing.

TO MAKE THE DYE. You will need ½ to one pound of onion skins to dye a pound of wool, depending upon the depth of color wanted. If you despair of ever saving that many onion skins from your own cooking, try collecting them from produce departments of grocery stores. Cover the onion skins with water and boil for 20 minutes. Cool and strain into the dyepot. Then add enough cold water to make 4 gallons.

BURNT ORANGE. Use alum-mordanted wool. Rinse mordanted wool thoroughly, and place the wet wool in the dyebath. Bring it gradually to a boil, and simmer it for half an hour. Let cool slightly, squeeze the excess moisture out of the wool, and rinse the dyed wool several times in water of decreasing temperatures. Press the skeins in an old but clean towel to dry them, and then hang out to dry in a shady place.

BRASS. Use chrome mordanted wool. *Right* after mordanting the wool, rinse it in water as warm as the mordant solution, then immerse the wool in the dyebath, which has been heated to the same temperature as the rinse water. Bring it gradually to a boil, and follow the same procedure as above.

Using Marigold Flowers to Obtain Yellow and Brass

TO MAKE THE DYE. Recycle the marigolds in your windowboxes by using them for dyeing! Use one peck of fresh flower heads, or ½ peck of dried flower heads. Cover the flowers with cold water and boil for half an hour. Let cool, strain into the dyepot, and add enough cold water to make 4 gallons.

YELLOW. Use alum-mordanted wool. Rinse the wool thoroughly, immerse it in the dyebath, and bring gradually to a boil. Simmer for one half to one hour until the desired color has been reached (wool appears darker when wet). Cool slightly, rinse several times in water of decreasing temperatures, and dry.

BRASS. Use chrome-mordanted wool. Right after mordanting the wool, rinse it in water as warm as the mordant solution, then immerse the wool in the dyebath, which has been heated to the same temperature as the rinse water. Bring gradually to a boil and follow the same procedure as above.

TO MAKE THE DYE. Any kind of fern will do. Use a pound of young "fiddleheads" (the coiled, immature ferns) or two pounds of mature ferns. Cover with water, bring to a boil, and simmer for two hours. Strain and add water to make 4 gallons.

YELLOW—GREEN. Use alum or chrome mordant. Immerse thoroughly rinsed and wetted mordanted wool into the dyepot, bring gradually to a boil, and simmer for one hour. Let it cool slightly, rinse several times in water of decreasing temperatures, and dry. To get a brighter color, try **66** adding a cup of household ammonia to the dyebath.

Using Tea Leaves to Obtain Tan and Light Brown

TO MAKE THE DYE. Cover ½ pound of black tea leaves with water, boil for 15 minutes, strain, and add cold water to make 4 gallons.

TAN. Use alum mordant. Rinse the mordanted wool thoroughly and throw the wet skeins into the dyebath. Bring it to a boil and let it simmer for half an hour. Cool slightly, and rinse repeatedly in water of decreasing temperatures, then hang in a shady place to dry.

LIGHT BROWN. Use chrome mordanted wool directly after the mordanting process, rinse it thoroughly, and follow the above procedure.

Using Goldenrod to Obtain Yellowish-Brown and Dark Gold

Dyeing

TO MAKE THE DYE. Pick the flowers just as they are starting to bloom. You will need one peck of fresh goldenrod flowers, or ½ peck of dried flowers. Cover them with cold water, bring to a boil, and boil for 45 minutes or so. Cool, strain, and add enough water to make 4 gallons.

YELLOWISH-BROWN. Use alum-mordanted wool. Immerse thoroughly rinsed and wetted wool into the dyebath, bring to a gradual boil, and simmer for one hour. Without rinsing the wool, place it into a second pot containing a boiling solution of 4 gallons of water, one teaspoon (¹/₆ ounce) of chrome and 6 tablespoons of vinegar. Simmer for 15 minutes, cool slightly, and rinse repeatedly in water of decreasing temperatures. Then hang it out to dry.

DARK GOLD. Use chrome-mordanted wool directly after mordanting. Rinse wool thoroughly in water as warm as the mordant solution, then immerse the wool in the dyebath, which has been heated to the same temperature as the last rinse water. Heat to boiling and simmer for 45 minutes. Let it cool slightly, then rinse and dry as above.

5 Learning on the Frame Loom

A frame loom is a basic loom. It consists mostly of a structure that keeps warp yarn taut and in order. Sometimes a frame loom can be embellished with harnesses or other helpful devices, but its beauty is in its simplicity. Any shape will do. Embroidery hoops, window frames, bicycle wheel frames, clothes hangers, jig saws, Tinker Toys, and even tree branches can become looms producing one-of-a-kind weavings. Or you can easily build one to fit the exact size and shape of the web you want to weave.

A frame loom is good for learning. The slow, deliberate pace of weaving on one encourages understanding of basic weaving concepts. It is an intimate loom. You are very much a part of it and control the weaving process with tools no more complicated than your fingers or a wooden ruler. Because of this closeness to the loom, and because there are no mysterious loom mechanisms, you can experience weaving with all of your senses. You clearly feel, touch, and see the relationship of warp to weft. You can readily understand and cope with problems of spacing, tension, and beating. And weaving on a frame loom is quiet. There is no noisy clatter as with more complex looms.

Frame looms have certain limitations—the fixed size of the web, the somewhat confining two harnesses, and the slowness of weaving. But they are especially useful because of their low cost, simplicity, and portability. Most frame looms require little floor space (you can prop one on a chair or table while weaving) and are small enough to tuck away in a closet or drawer when you have finished weaving for the day. And you can weave on a frame loom almost anywhere. Take it to a friend's house, or outside in the shade of a tree, or set it up on the kitchen table while your bread is baking!

The usual two-harness construction of frame looms restricts weavers to the *tabby* or *plain* weave, rather than the more complex threadings possible on multiple-harness looms. This limitation can be used to advantage, however, as it forces an in-depth exploration of the tabby weave, which is the simple over-and-under interlacing of warp and weft. By using varying sizes and colors of yarns, by skipping warp spaces, beating unevenly, or by using knotting and tapestry techniques, it is easy to see that the possibilities of creativity with the tabby weave are endless.

Figure 5.1 Tabby weave.

The static weaving space of frame looms determines the size of the web. There is comparatively little waste of warp ends, but because of this rigid size, identical items must be woven separately rather than in a running length. To weave six place mats, you have to set up the loom six times. This is time-consuming and tedious for an impatient person. There are more elaborate small looms available, however, which can accomodate longer warps by means of rolling beams.

It is wise, when learning any craft, to begin with the most basic tools. Just as it wouldn't be logical to buy a tractor for your first garden plot, or a yacht for learning to sail, it is not a good idea to start weaving on a four-harness floor loom. Most larger looms and equipment are very cumbersome and expensive. Before spending a lot of money on complex weaving tools, spend some time with a frame loom. You will learn weaving "from scratch" through your experiments with it, and you'll get a solid background and some self-confidence before going on to larger looms.

BUYING FRAME LOOMS

There is a bewildering assortment of frame looms for sale in craft stores, supply houses, hobby shops, schools, and museums. When you think about buying a frame loom, it is important to decide whether you want one that is merely practical or one that is also beautiful. Remember, you will pay extra for looks! Sturdy metal-frame looms are workable and reasonably priced. Handmade wooden looms with two, three, or even four harnesses are decorative and wonderful to weave on but can cost a lot.

Or you can make your own frame loom! When learning how to weave, constructing your first tools will give a very basic understanding of the fundamentals. And it's exciting when a jumble of boards, string, and yarn actually evolves into a working loom producing fabric. It doesn't have to be fancy; you might be happy at first experimenting with looms from your environment—the tree branch or embroidery hoop. But for our first two weaving projects, we will construct a simple but effective frame loom that has a few advantages over these "found" looms. It is sturdy, permanent, a convenient size, easy to build, and costs very little.

A FRAME LOOM TO MAKE YOURSELF

This simple loom consists of a canvas stretcher frame, a dowel harness with string heddles (alternate warp ends are threaded through the heddles), and a ruler harness. It is 22" by 30" and is designed to weave a web 16" by 22" or smaller. You will need a set of canvas stretchers 22" by 30" (available at any art store), a staple gun or four L-shaped brackets, one wooden dowel ½" by 22," and one yardstick (or similar flat stick) cut to 18" long.

Assemble the frame from the canvas stretchers. Secure the corners with the staple gun or L-shaped brackets. And that's all there is to it! The dowel harness, string heddles, and ruler harness, will be mounted on the loom after the warp is wound on. You are now ready to weave.

PROJECT 1—STRIPED HANDBAG (Tabby weave, weft faced)

PLANNING AND DESIGN

This woven shoulder bag is made of a folded single 10"-by-22" web. It is woven in **weft-faced weave**, the warp completely covered by the weft. This is done by spacing the warp yarn very widely and beating the weft hard. The bag can be many-colored and textured with different yarns; at least two weft colors should be used to give interest to the design.

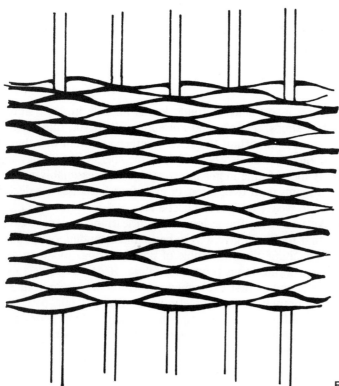

Figure 5.2 Weft-faced tabby weave.

Warp

The warp should be a strong, medium-weight, smooth yarn with little give or elasticity. Ordinary cotton string or jute twine from the hardware store are fine. Don't use a furry or hairy yarn. The warp color doesn't matter as it will be covered by the weft, and will only show if you leave the knotted fringe showing. You will need about 75 yards of warp.

74

Weft

This is where you can have some fun. Almost any type of yarn can be used for the weft. Medium weight to heavy soft yarns are best for the strength and bulk you want in a bag. Wool, synthetics, heavy cottons, alpaca, mohair, or a combination of fibers, can be used. Odds and ends of knitting yarns are fine, too. Or, if you have been learning to spin or dye, here is an opportunity to use up your early efforts! Even irregular handspun yarn will give a handsome texture. If you can't scrounge any yarn and are hesitant about buying expensive fibers, try the local dimestore for wool blends or synthetic sport yarn.

Color

The most important thing about choosing colors is that you like them. If a color combination of fibers pleases you, no doubt you will be satisfied with the finished woven effect. In making a handbag such as this one, gaudy multicolored stripes can be very attractive, as it is a small compactly woven area. Two dull colors, such as black and grey and a contrasting color such as red, will also harmonize well. If you are totally uninspired, refer to nature for the best coloring ideas. The dappled browns and golds of a forest floor, the startling marking of a butterfly, or the subtle tones of an interesting rock are all suggestive of sound color schemes for weaving. Never be afraid to try anything in weaving—if it doesn't work, you can always rip it out!

SETTING UP THE LOOM

Winding on the warp

There is no premeasuring of warp ends on this frame loom. The warp is wound directly on the loom in a figure-eight fashion. Fasten the warp yarn with a knot around the top beam at the upper left. Draw the warp under the lower beam, around and over the lower beam; up and under the top beam, around and over the top beam, and so on. Wind it on rather tightly and keep it evenly stretched. Continue until there are the right number of warp ends on the loom. Tie off the warp at the right tension beam and adjust the width of the warp at both top and bottom to 10." To calculate the right number of warp ends for this project, multiply the number of ends per inch (**e.p.i.**) by 10. If you will be using medium to fine weft yarns, a good e.p.i. is 6 ends per inch; the total number of warp ends is 60. If you will be using very bulky weft yarns, your e.p.i. will be 4 or even 3 ends per

Figure 5.3 Winding on the warp.

77

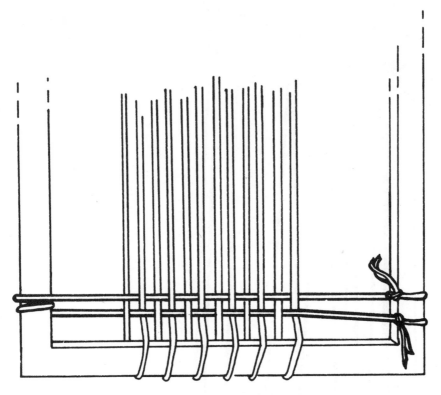

Figure 5.4 Weaving two rows at the top and the bottom to secure the warp.

inch; the total number of ends will be 40 or 30. Remember, the warp is spaced very widely so that the weft can be beaten down closely and will completely cover the warp.

To keep the warp ends evenly spaced and in order, tie a length of warp yarn to the left side support just below the top beam, weaving in and out of the warp ends; turn around the right side support, weave back again, in and out, the alternate warp ends and tie them to the left side support. Weave two rows of yarn in the same way just above the lower beam. Make sure the warp covers 10" on both the the top and lower beams.

Securing the String Heddles

With the loom on a flat surface, place the dowel across the center, resting the ends on the loom side supports. Tie some lengths of string or twine along the length of the dowel. Wind a small ball of string or twine and tie it **78** to the left side of the dowel. Bring the string under the *first* warp end; bring

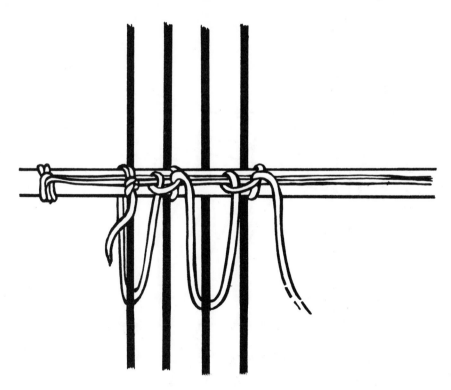

Figure 5.5 Tying on the string heddles.

it behind the dowel, make a loop around the lengths of string tied along the dowel, then tie a half-hitch around the dowel, as shown. This is one string heddle. Bring the string under the *third* warp end; bring it up behind the dowel and make another loop and half-hitch. Continue in this way across the dowel, looping around *every other* warp end and securing the string around the dowel in between each heddle. Keep the loops as even in length as you can. At the right side of the dowel, make a knot and cut the string. Lift the dowel; the loops, or heddles, will lift every other warp end, making the **shed**, or space for the weft yarn to pass through.

Inserting the Second Harness

Place the 18" length of wooden yardstick under the second, fourth, and sixth warp ends. Continue across the entire warp. When the stick is turned on its side, the second shed is formed.

79

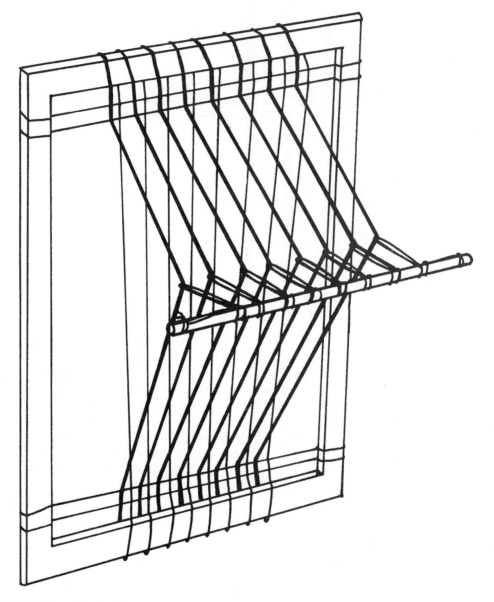

Figure 5.6 The shed formed by dowel
harness and string heddles.

80

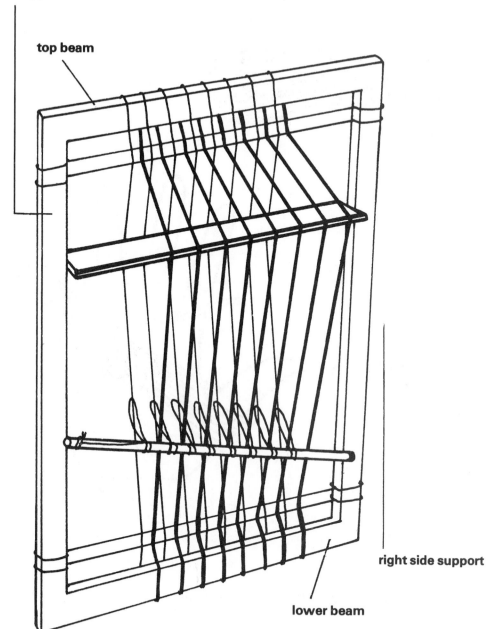

left side support

top beam

right side support

lower beam

Figure 5.7 The shed formed by ruler harness.

81

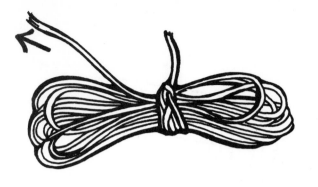

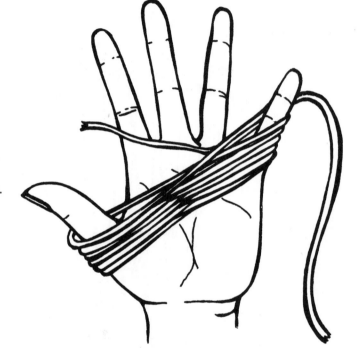

Figure 5.8 A butterfly hand bobbin.

Making a Butterfly Hand Bobbin

Make a butterfly bobbin with one color of yarn. Wind the yarn repeatedly in a figure eight around your thumb and little finger as shown; then take the wound yarn off your hand carefully and tie it firmly around the middle. Notice that the yarn will pull out evenly from the center of the butterfly for ease in weaving.

Beginning to Weave

Turn the ruler on its edge. Pass the butterfly through the shed from right to left, leaving 3 or 4 inches at the right. Bring this end around the last warp on the right and tuck it back into the shed. One row of weaving is called a *pick*.

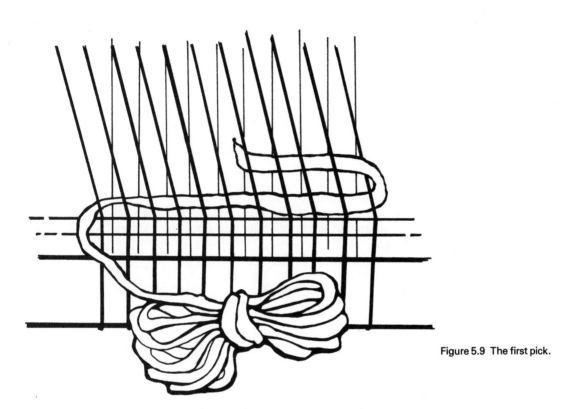

Figure 5.9 The first pick.

Beating the Weft

Turn the ruler flat. With a table fork, comb, tapestry beater, or your fingers, press the weft yarn down firmly, all across the pick. This is called *beating*.

Raising the String Heddles

Push the ruler to the *top* of the warp. Lift up the dowel and pass the butterfly through the new shed, diagonally to give a bit of slack. Release the dowel harness and beat the weft down with the fork. Slide down the ruler harness, turn it on its edge, and pass the butterfly back through the shed to the left, diagonally, beating the weft as before. Check to see that the warp is being completely covered by the weft. If it is not, the weft yarn is too thick for the number of ends per inch. Use a finer yarn, or spread the warp out a bit (this will make the fabric wider.) Continue weaving until the color stripe is wide enough for your taste, or until the butterfly runs out.

Ending the Old Weft and Starting the New

At the end of the last row of a color, bring the weft yarn around the last warp end, and back into the shed. Beat as before. Start the new weft as in the beginning but at the opposite side from the ending of the last weft (to avoid bulges).

Watching your Weaving

As you continue to weave, try to keep the edges, or *selvedges,* from being pulled in. Allow enough slack by passing the weft through the shed diagonally. If loops form at the selvedges, you are giving the weft too much slack. With practice, you will find the best method of selvedge control.

Be sure that the warp ends are covered, by careful and firm beating of the weft. As you weave, experiment with colors and textures. Follow a stripe of very bulky yarn with a width of finer yarn; contrast smooth textures with fuzzy or lumpy ones.

When you have woven most of the 22" web, you will find that the sheds have become smaller; it will be easier to weave in the last few inches with a yarn needle. When the web is 22" long, finish off the last color as before. Cut the warp from the loom across the top beam and the lower beam.

Finishing

Tie a simple knotted fringe across the top and bottom of the web, with four warp ends for each knot. This fringe can be left as it is or folded under and hemmed.

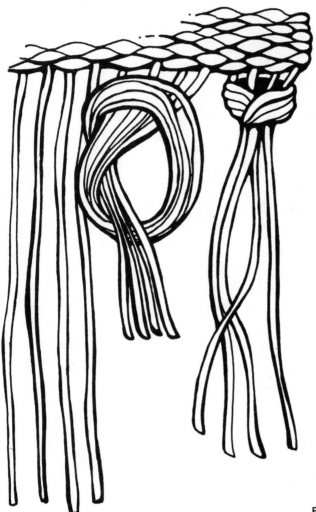

Figure 5.10 Knotting the fringe.

Fold the web in half, and sew the sides with a chain stitch as shown, using a yarn needle with doubled yarn. The handle can be crocheted, knotted, or braided in any length. Knot the ends of the handle at the sides of the pocketbook.

PROJECT 2—WALL HANGING (Tabby weave, weft faced. Ghiordes knotting technique)

PLANNING AND DESIGN

This 10"-by-14" hanging will be woven in weft-faced tabby weave, textured with rows of *Ghiordes* (pronounced *yor-deez*) knotting, using the *rya* technique (with precut knotting ends.) The finished web will hang from a stick or dowel and will have a simple fringe on both top and bottom.

Warp

Use a medium-weight warp fiber; jute, string, or heavy linen are especially effective.

Weft

Medium to heavy yarns are good, and textured fibers such as handspun yarns will give the hanging depth and interest. For the knotting technique, try soft, thick, or hairy yarns.

Colors

It's a good idea to limit yourself to three colors to emphasize the textural interest of the hanging. These can be contrasting colors or different tones of one color. For instance, a natural brown warp, beige weft, and off-white knotted yarn would be a subtle accent on a wall. Or make a vivid hanging in a bright combination such as black, white, and orange.

SETTING UP THE LOOM

Wind the warp on the loom as in Project 1, figuring out the number of warp ends as before, with the addition of one extra warp end for even spacing of the knots. Weave two lengths of yarn at the top and bottom of the warp as before. Tie the string heddles on the dowel stick and insert the ruler for the second harness as before.

WEAVING

Make a butterfly of weft yarn and weave 8 inches, paying close attention to even selvedges and firm beating. End the weft as before, tucking it back into the last shed.

87

88

Wind the yarn you have chosen for knotting around a piece of cardboard 4" long, about 20 times or so. Cut across the yarn at one end of the cardboard to make 8" ends for knotting. Start the first row of knots as follows: tie a knot around the first two warp ends as shown. Pull the ends down, securing the knot. Skip one warp end and tie the second knot around the next two ends. Skip one warp end and continue in this way across the row. After this first row of knots, weave one inch of weft as before, then tie another row of knots, cutting more 8" lengths of knotting yarn as you need it. If you want a fuller knotted fringe, double the knotting ends together and treat two as one end. Or rows of knotting can be separated by as little as one pick of regular weaving.

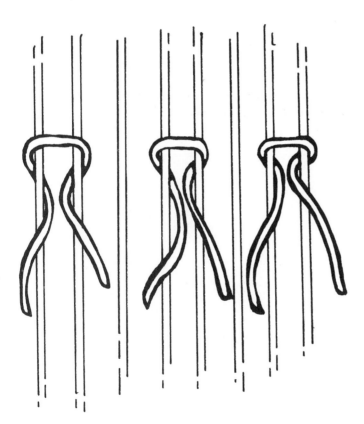

Figure 5.11 The Ghiordes knot.

Four rows of knots, separated by one-inch widths of warp-faced tabby weave, make an effective hanging. But make as many rows as you want, and complete the web with three inches of weft-faced weaving.

Finishing

Cut the web from the loom and make simple knotted fringes at the top and bottom. Cut the Ghiordes-knotted ends evenly if you wish. You can tie wooden or ceramic beads or shells to the lower fringe.

SOME OTHER IDEAS FOR WEAVING ON A FRAME LOOM

Place mats, 12"-by-18", can be woven from a variety of fibers, such as raffia, grasses, string, cotton, plastic or synthetic cording, as well as cotton and linen.

Napkins, 12"-by-12", should be woven of washable fibers, such as cottons, linens, or synthetics.

Piece 12"-by-12" squares together to make skirts, afghans, ponchos, and scarves.

Rugs can be made by piecing together squares or rectangles of woven fabric closely knotted in the Ghiordes technique.

6 Recipes for Weaving

There is only one way to set up a frame loom such as we have been using—the warp is wound onto the frame in a figure-eight fashion and two harnesses raise alternate warp ends, creating two sheds. We have seen that the only type of weave possible on this loom is the plain or *tabby* weave. When there are more harnesses on a loom, however, many weaves can be created by threading the warp in different ways and by raising the harnesses in various sequences. To understand a weave pattern, to plan a project with a certain weave, and to avoid confusion and mistakes while weaving, it is necessary to write out a "recipe" for the pattern. Recipes for weaving are called *drafts*.

WRITING A DRAFT FOR A TABBY WEAVE

Drafts are written with a kind of shorthand weaving language on graph paper. The symbols in this language can vary among different centuries, **91** countries, and even individual weavers. There are, however, certain similarities in drafts, and if you thoroughly understand the fairly standard modern draft which we will look at in this chapter, you will be able to figure out most other kinds of drafts.

ON A TWO-HARNESS LOOM

There are three parts of a draft: the *threading,* the *tie-up,* and the *draw-down.* Only one section of the weaving is diagrammed in a draft; this section is to be repeated across the width of the warp while setting up a loom. To learn how to write drafts, let's look at the simple drafts for the tabby weave as woven on both a two-harness frame loom and a four-harness loom.

There are many ways to vary a tabby weave. In the last chapter we used weft-faced weaves and added weft stripes and knotting; other variations include warp-faced weaves, warp stripes, and finger-manipulated weaves (those controlled by the weaver rather than the threading of the loom). But in all of these tabby weaves, the construction of the fabric is the same; the weft threads pass over and under the warp ends on one pick or row, and under and over the warp ends on the next pick.

The first part of a draft is the *threading draft,* which indicates how the warp is threaded through the harnesses. A threading draft is written and read from *right to left.* On the frame loom, the first harness was a dowel with string heddles lifting every other warp end. The ruler lifted the rest of the warp ends. The threading draft shows this: each square symbolizes one warp end; the numbers refer to the harnesses through which they pass.

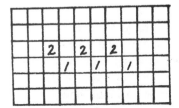

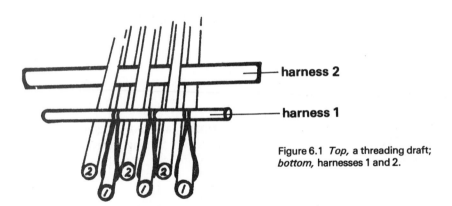

harness 2

harness 1

Figure 6.1 *Top,* a threading draft; *bottom,* harnesses 1 and 2.

The *draw-down* in a draft, which reads from top to bottom, shows the construction of the woven fabric. Each horizontal row of the draw-down represents one pick of weft. Each filled-in square in a draw-down represents the weft as it goes *over* the warp ends; each blank square shows where the warp is raised by a harness and the weft passes *under* the warp. To make a draw-down, imagine that you are raising the harnesses, threaded as in the threading draft, and passing the weft through the shed. Fill in the squares that the weft passes over. In the first pick, harness 1 is raised and the

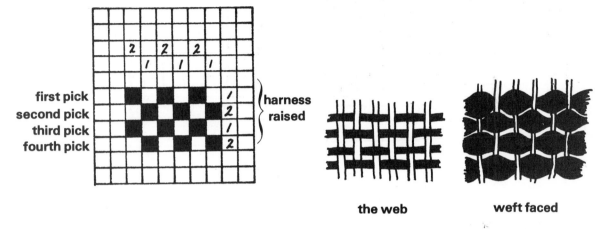

Figure 6.2 Threading draft and draw-down.

weft passes through the shed, going over the filled-in squares. Notice that even with the weft-faced tabby weave that we used in Projects 1 and 2, the construction of the fabric follows this draft draw-down.

ON A FOUR-HARNESS FLOOR LOOM

The harnesses on a four-harness loom contain heddles made of wire or string through which the warp ends are threaded. The harnesses are numbered from the front of the loom to the back.

A tabby weave is set up on a four-harness loom by dividing the warp ends equally among the four harnesses; every other warp end (for instance, the *odd* ends) must be raised in the first shed, and all the even ends raised in the second shed. To produce these alternate sheds with the ends equally divided between the harnesses, the loom is threaded as follows: the first warp end (on the right) is threaded through a heddle on the first (odd) harness; the second warp end is threaded through a heddle on the second (even) harness; the third warp end is threaded through a heddle on the third (odd) harness; the fourth warp end is threaded through a heddle on the fourth (even) harness. This sequence is repeated across the width of the warp.

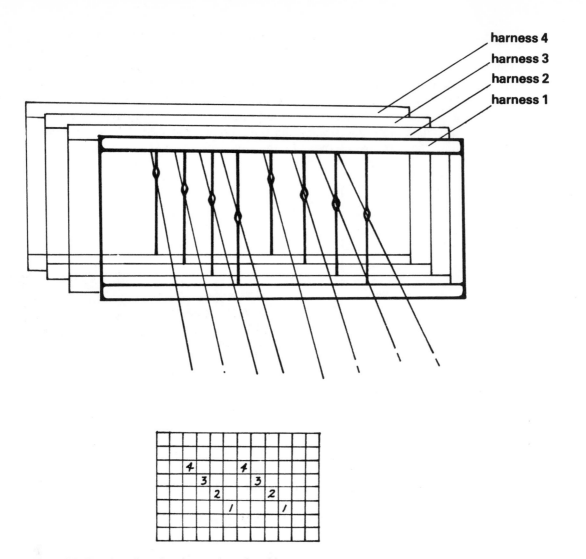

Figure 6.3 *Top,* threading a four-harness loom for tabby weave; *bottom,* threading draft.

When the first and third harnesses are raised, all the odd warp ends will be raised; the second and fourth harnesses will raise all the even warp ends.

The *tie-up* specifies the way the harnesses are attached to the treadles of a multiple-harness loom. Harnesses are actually attached to horizontal sticks called *lams,* and the differences in tying take place between the lams **94** and the treadles.

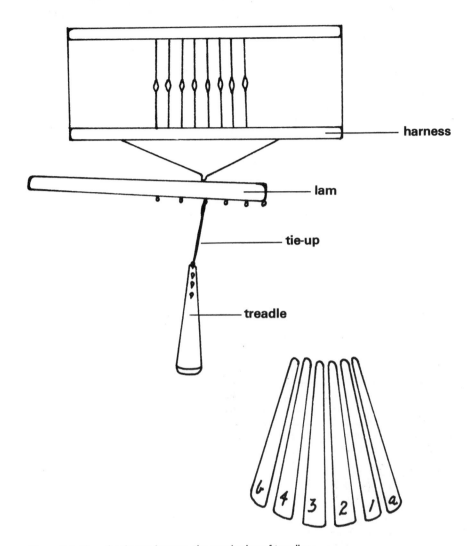

— harness

— lam

— tie-up

— treadle

Figure 6.4 *Top,* the tie-up; *bottom,* the numbering of treadles.

Treadles are numbered as shown; the treadle on the far right is treadle *a* and the one on the far left is *b.* Treadles 1, 2, 3 and 4 are numbered consecutively from right to left.

For the tabby weave, tie harnesses 1 and 3 to treadle *a;* tie harnesses 2 and 4 to treadle *b.*

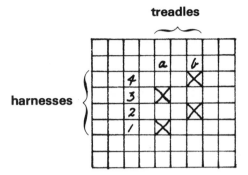

treadles

harnesses

Figure 6.5 The tie-up.

For writing a draft of the draw-down of the tabby weave on a four-harness loom, try to visualize what is happening on the loom. For the first pick, treadle *a* is stepped on, raising harnesses 1 and 3; the weft passes under all the odd warp ends. With the next pick, treadle *b* raises harnesses 2 and 4; the weft passes under all the even warp ends.

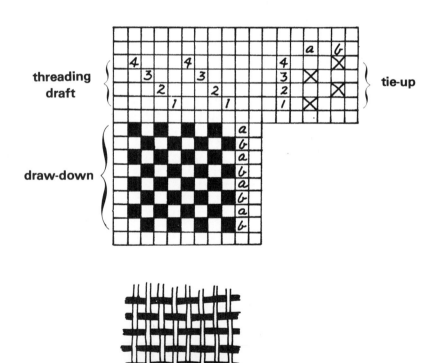

threading draft

tie-up

draw-down

Figure 6.6 *Top,* complete draft of four-harness tabby weave; *bottom,* diagram of tabby weave.

96

WRITING A DRAFT FOR A TWILL WEAVE

There are three kinds of weave structures from which all other weaves are derived: tabby, twill, and satin. As a true satin weave must be woven with at least five harnesses, we won't examine it in this book. We have already looked at the over-and-under structure of the tabby weave. In a *twill,* the weft which passes over the warp in one pick does not lie directly over the next visible weft below it. This staggered construction of twill weaves appears as diagonals in the woven fabric.

Figure 6.7 *Top,* twill fabric; *bottom,* diagram of plain twill.

Twill can be threaded on three harnesses, but for purposes of comparison with the four-harness tabby weave, we will use the more common four-harness twill. For a draft of a plain twill, the threading is the same as for a tabby weave.

97

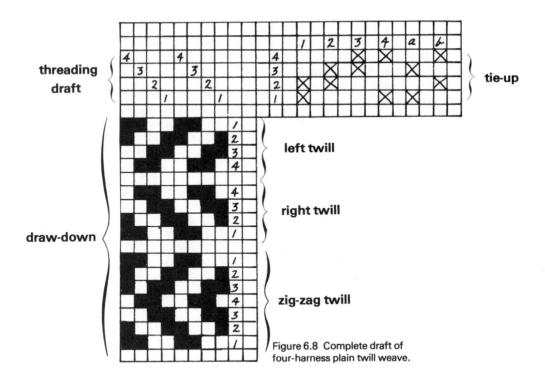

threading draft

tie-up

left twill

right twill

draw-down

zig-zag twill

Figure 6.8 Complete draft of four-harness plain twill weave.

The tie-up for this twill weave is known as a standard or a *direct tie-up*. Treadle 1 is tied to harnesses 1 and 2; treadle 2 is tied to harnesses 2 and 3; treadle 3 is tied to harnesses 3 and 4; treadle 4 is tied to harnesses 4 and 1. As for the tabby weave, treadle *a* is tied to harnesses 1 and 3; treadle *b* to harnesses 2 and 4. This direct tie-up, and the threading sequence, can be used for both tabby and twill. The treadling is what makes the difference in the appearance of the woven fabric.

As you can see in the draw-down, the weft passes under two adjacent warp ends, over two warp ends, under two warp ends, and so on. In the next pick the weft first goes under two warp ends, one of which it went under in the first pick. This creates a strong fabric with the characteristic twill diagonals. Three different treadlings of the plain twill are shown.

SOME OTHER WEAVES

TABBY

You can weave an infinite variety of tabby fabrics from the same draft. In weaving a weft-faced tabby, such as Projects 1 and 2 on the frame **98** loom, we used widely sleyed warp ends. To make a warp-faced fabric, the warp must be sleyed closely. A 50/50 tabby web has, ideally, the same number of warp ends per inch as weft picks. You can vary tabby weaving by changing the relative size of warp to weft and by the use of colors, stripes, and various tapestry techniques (see chapter 7, Project 4). Uneven sleying and irregular beating also change the character of tabby cloth.

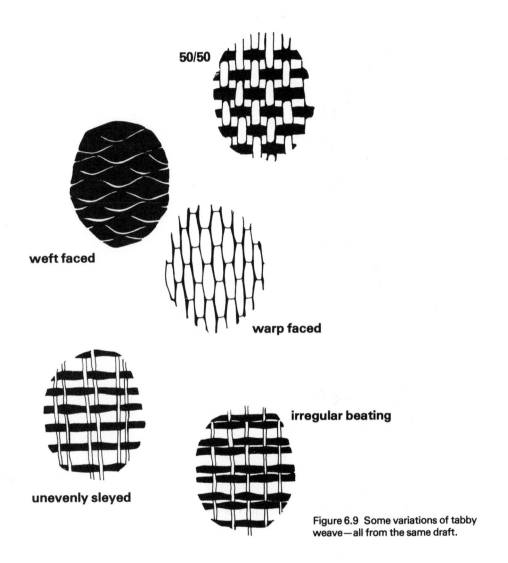

50/50

weft faced

warp faced

unevenly sleyed

irregular beating

Figure 6.9 Some variations of tabby weave—all from the same draft.

A derivative of the tabby weave, using groups of warp ends and weft picks, is called the *basket weave*. Note the difference in the tie-up. As you can see by the draw-down, it can be combined in the same web with a tabby weave. Basket weave is used for weaving table linens, blankets, coat material, and for other sturdy fabrics.

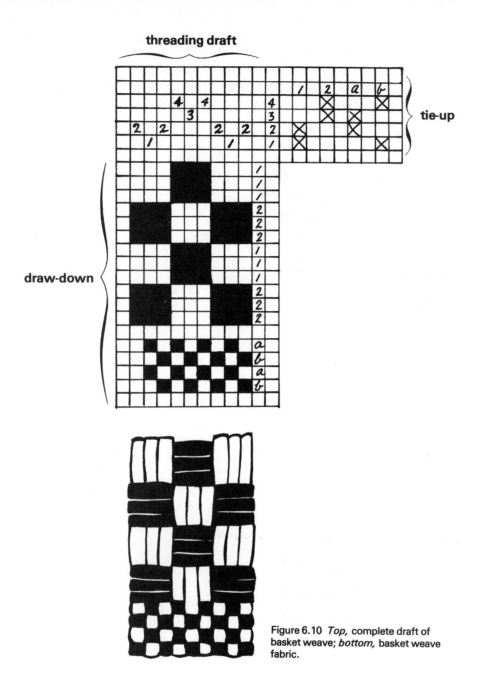

threading draft

tie-up

draw-down

Figure 6.10 *Top,* complete draft of basket weave; *bottom,* basket weave fabric.

TWILL

Twill weaves have all the versatility of tabby weaves, and more! Very interesting things can happen when you weave warp-faced or weft-faced **100** twills. And because the direct tie-up and threading for twill is the same as for tabby, the two weaves can be combined on the same web by using different treadling. There seems to be a twill weave for every use. We have already seen the draft for plain twill; two other types of twill are the *return* or *point twill* and *broken twill*, which will be used in Project 5.

When you look at the threading draft for a point twill, the reason for the name becomes obvious.

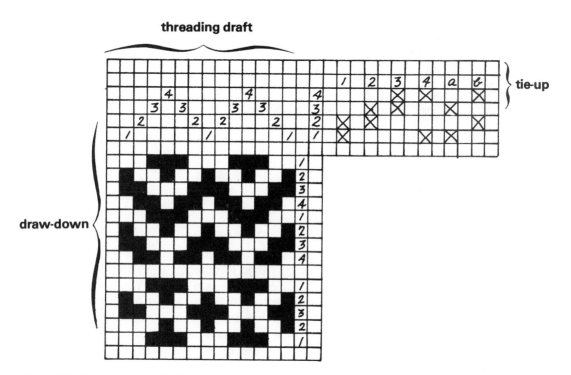

Figure 6.11 Complete draft of bird's eye point twill.

This *bird's eye* point twill, like all twills, can be treadled in a great many ways. When you first set up the loom in a twill pattern, make a sampler with as many kinds of treadling as you can devise. Just two sequences are shown in this draw-down; another version appears in Project 6.

Rosepath is the name given to a very popular point twill used in weaving everything from skirt material to dish towels. Since a direct tie-up is used, you can weave a rosepath border on a plain tabby web.

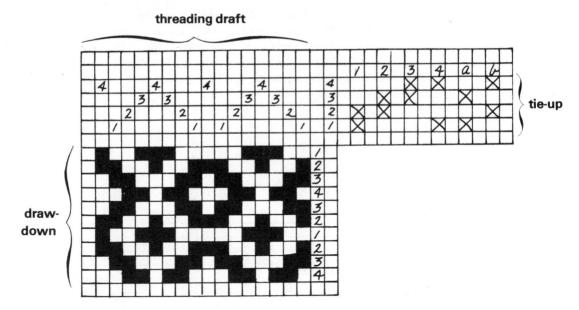

threading draft

tie-up

draw-down

Figure 6.12 Complete draft of rosepath point twill.

Again, you can think up all kinds of treadling for rosepath weaves; and, frequently, a pattern thread is used in addition to a tabby thread. This is a very effective technique used in many other weaves, particularly *overshot,* which we will look at next; but it helps to get used to it in a simpler weave such as this one. The tabby thread uses the *a,b,a,b* treadling of the tabby weave—*one pick in between each pick of the pattern thread* that uses a twill treadling. A draw-down, and instructions in most weaving books, will not mention separate treadling directions for the tabby thread. Weaving sequence for the first part of the treadling shown in this draw-down would be:

treadle 1 with pattern thread,

treadle *a* with tabby thread,

treadle 2 with pattern thread

treadle *b* with tabby thread,

treadle 3 with pattern thread,

102   treadle *a* with tabby thread,

treadle 4 with pattern thread,

treadle *b* with tabby thread.

Another type of twill, *broken twill,* can be seen in Project 5.

OVERSHOT

The lovely, intricate coverlets of colonial days were woven in *overshot weaves.* An overshot fabric appears to be a tabby web with pattern threads forming designs on its surface. The structure of the fabric is, however, an offshoot of twill, which you can see by studying the threading draft and tie-up. Weaving overshot is not difficult, although the threading of the loom may take a bit longer. There are quite a few books around with countless drafts for overshot, which can be used with either a traditional or a modern approach. Overshot is generally woven as a 50/50 web, although patterns can be given an interesting appearance with varied sleying, beating, and yarns. For the pattern thread in an overshot, treadle as indicated in the draw-down. For the tabby, treadle *a,b,a,b* between each pick of pattern thread.

Snail's trail is a common overshot pattern, shown here with an elongated character made by closer sleying. Another overshot pattern is outlined in Project 7, chapter 7. The treadling sequence for the pattern thread of snail's trail is as follows:

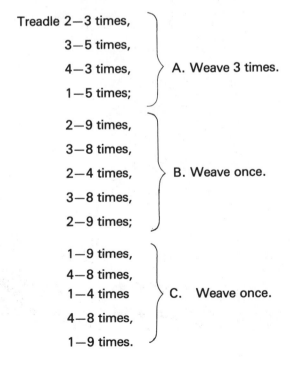

Treadle 2—3 times,

       3—5 times,

       4—3 times,   A. Weave 3 times.

       1—5 times;

       2—9 times,

       3—8 times,

       2—4 times,   B. Weave once.

       3—8 times,

       2—9 times;

       1—9 times,

       4—8 times,

       1—4 times   C. Weave once.

       4—8 times,

       1—9 times.

Figure 6.13 Snail's trail overshot in cupboard panels.

Recipes
for Weaving

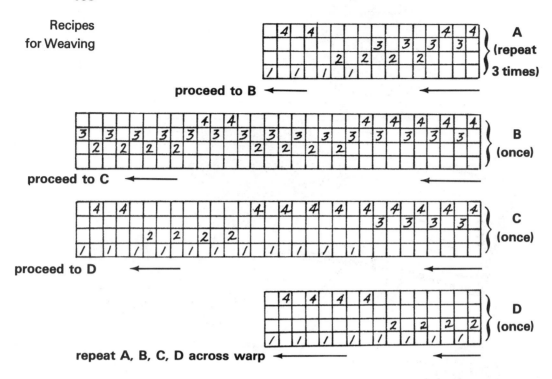

proceed to B ←

proceed to C ←

proceed to D ←

repeat A, B, C, D across warp ←

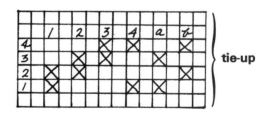

tie-up

Figure 6.14 *Top,* threading draft for snail's trail overshot; *bottom* tie-up.

Remember that this treadling refers to the pattern thread only. In between the picks of the pattern, treadle *a* or *b* with picks of tabby thread.

When you have become familiar with setting up your loom and with the simpler weaves, try some of the countless patterns and drafts described in this and in other weaving books (see chapter 9). Soon you will understand drafting and the structure of weaves well enough to design your own fabrics completely!

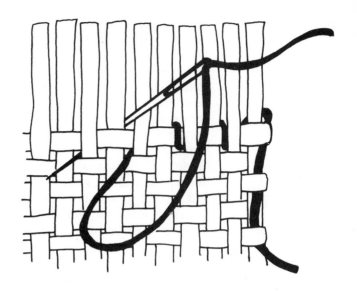

7 The Four-Harness Loom

The frame loom we have been using has two harnesses—the dowel and the ruler. We have seen how the two harnesses, which lift different warp ends, restrict the weaver to certain weave patterns. As more harnesses are added to a loom structure, greater varieties of weaves are possible (see chapter 6, "Recipes for Weaving"). Looms for home use can have up to sixteen harnesses, but for most handweavers a four-harness loom is ideal. With four harnesses you can design enough different patterns to keep you busy for a very long time! And when you think of all the yarns, textures and colors there are, it is easy to see the creative possibilities of weaving on a four-harness loom.

TYPES OF FOUR-HARNESS LOOMS

Four-harness *table looms* have the same basic structure as four-harness *floor looms*. The main difference is that the harnesses are controlled by hand levers on table looms and by foot pedals or treadles on floor looms. Table looms are smaller than floor looms—an advantage in storage and weaving space but a disadvantage in the narrower web. In this book, we will work with the popular floor loom. If you can weave on a floor loom, you'll be able to understand the workings of any other loom.

Floor looms are big, heavy, and usually expensive pieces of equipment. Before buying one, read up on different weaves and send for catalogs describing different looms. If you're interested in very complex weaves, for instance, perhaps you should buy a loom with room for eight or sixteen harnesses that can be added in the future. How mobile are you? Some looms can fold up for easy moving and storage, while some have to be completely disassembled to fit through a doorway. Try out as many looms as you can, and ask weaving friends their preferences. Looms are one of the last real bargains around! They may cost a lot initially, but most looms are extremely well-built, and will last a lifetime.

Every weaver has his own ideas about loom performance, so don't let differing opinions confuse you. All loom types and individual looms have their good points; find the one that suits *you* best.

There are three types of floor looms: jack looms, counterbalanced looms, and *contre-marche* looms. Each type has a different way of forming the shed for the weft to pass through.

Jack looms, now the most common in the United States, form a shed by *lifting up* some warp ends from the rest, which remain *stationary*. The greatest advantage of a jack loom is that you can weave patterns with *unbalanced treadling,* such as raising first one harness and then three at once. Some weavers object to the uneven weaving tension in jack looms; the warp ends being raised are stretched more tautly than the others. Jack looms are the noisiest looms, but any loom will produce some clanking and thumping.

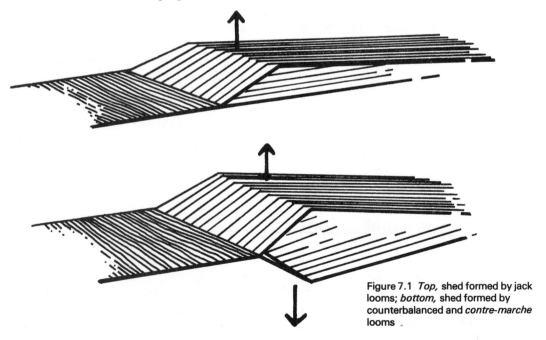

Figure 7.1 *Top,* shed formed by jack looms; *bottom,* shed formed by counterbalanced and *contre-marche* looms .

Counterbalanced looms raise selected warp ends while simultaneously *lowering* the rest. This method of forming a shed gives equal tension to all the warp ends at once. Counterbalanced harnesses are hung from the top of the loom and work in pairs. Unbalanced treadling is therefore not very successful; sometimes a web can be woven upside-down or compensation can be made in the tie-up, but for certain patterns the counterbalanced loom simply won't work.

Contre-marche looms have long been favored by Scandinavian weavers, and are becoming more popular and readily available in the United States. *Contre-marche* looms form a shed in the same way as counterbalanced looms, but their construction allows unbalanced treadling.

PARTS OF THE LOOM

Whichever loom you choose to buy or to learn on, sit down with it, study its structure, and learn how it works. Looms of every type have the same basic parts, although they might be put together differently.

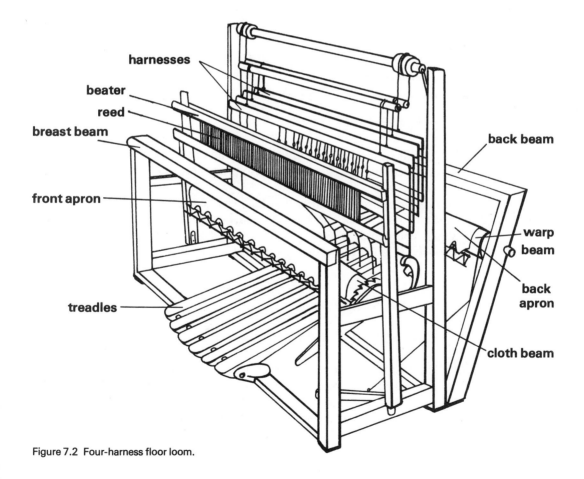

Figure 7.2 Four-harness floor loom.

On a frame loom, warp ends are kept taut by the rigid upper and lower beams. On a floor loom, warp ends are stretched over the front or *breast beam* and the *back beam*. Before being woven, the warp is wound around the *warp beam,* then passes over the back beam. After the weft has been woven onto the warp, the web passes over the front breast beam and is wound onto the *cloth beam.* The warp is tied to the *cloth aprons* attached to the back beam and the cloth beam.

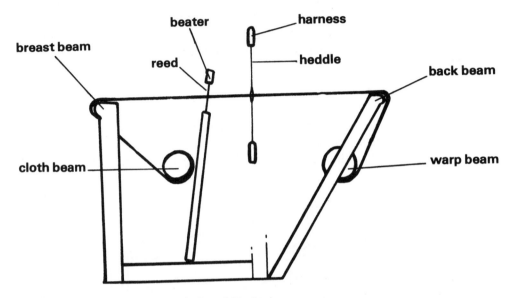

Figure 7.3 Diagram of one warp end on the loom (side view).

Warp ends are kept equally separated and in order by the *reed.* The reed is supported by the *beater,* which also presses each new pick of weft against the woven web.

The *harnesses* are frames that hold the *heddles.* Warp ends are threaded through the eyes of the heddles, which may be made of string or metal. When you depress a foot *treadle,* the attached harness lifts the warp ends threaded through its heddles and a shed is formed.

GETTING READY TO WEAVE

PLANNING AND DESIGN

The first step in any weaving project is to figure out what you are going to weave and how you will do it! You have to calculate how much yarn you will need and how you will thread the loom. A special notebook for describing each weaving project is a great help in planning and in recording your projects, especially if it includes samples of your weavings.

Article

In planning each weaving project, first decide what article you want to weave and how many you want to weave at once. You could weave two wall hangings at one time, or a blanket and cushion cover on a single warping. The setting-up of the warp is the longest part of the weaving process; save yourself some time in advance by weaving several things on one warp.

Size

Determine the *finished* size of each article and then the *total finished size* of all the articles. For instance, in Project 3, which is found later in this chapter, we will weave six place mats. Each place mat is a 12"-by-18" web, with one half inch of fringe at each end. The finished size of each place mat, then, is really 12" wide and 19" long. Multiply the 19" length by six (for the number of place mats you want) and you will find that the finished web, before cutting it into the six mats, will be 12" wide and 114" long.

Now you need to know how long the warp ends must be *on the loom* to produce a web of 114" in length. Allowance must be made for *loom waste,* which is extra warp used to set up the loom and which can't be woven. This is usually about 36". The warp, stretched taut while on a loom, will natually get shorter when removed from the loom. The extra length needed for this *take-up* varies according to the elasticity of the warp yarn. For a very elastic yarn such as wool or acrylic sport yarn, for example, allow an extra 6" of take-up per yard; for less elastic cotton or linen warp, use 3" per yard. You'll learn with experience how much take-up to allow with different warp yarns. Now, to figure out the length of warp needed for the six place mats in Project 3 :

> 114" for finished length of web
> 36" loom waste
> 24" take-up (6" times 3½ yards of the finished length)
> + _____
> 174" = 4 yards and 30" or, rounded off to the next higher yard,
>   5 yards.

The width of the warp will draw in a bit as it is being woven; allow one inch of drawing in for every 12" of width. The width of the web on the loom for Project 3 will be 12"+ 1"= 13." *The size of the warp on the loom will be 5 yards by 13."*

Warp yarn

Pick out the yarn you want for warp, referring to chapter 2, "Fibers," if you need to. The main thing to remember about warp is that it must be strong. If it breaks easily when you stretch it, it will drive you crazy on the loom! For Project 3, we will use a medium-weight synthetic yarn. It is very strong and practical for washable place mats.

Weft yarn

Again, refer to chapter 2 for suggestions about weft yarns and fibers. For Project 3, the same yarn is used for the weft as for the warp.

Sett

The *sett,* or *e.p.i.,* is the number of warp *ends per inch.* The warp ends are *sleyed,* or threaded, through the reed to hold them a certain distance apart. The sett is determined by the thickness of the warp yarn and the type of weave. With the frame loom we saw how wide sleying with the weft beaten down closely caused *weft-faced weaving.* If the warp and weft show equally, a *50/50 weave* is produced. A very closely sleyed warp will created a *warp-faced weave.*

In Project 3 we will plan for a 50/50 weave, although variations in yarns and beating may make it somewhat unbalanced. The sett will be 10 *e.p.i.*

Reeds come in different sizes. Each space for the yarn to pass through is called a *dent.* Eight-dent (8 dents per inch), 10-dent, 12-dent, and 15-dent reeds are the most common. The warp ends may be sleyed in each dent, in alternate dents, or in a staggered manner. They may be doubled in each dent or in every third dent, depending on the effect you want.

Number of warp ends

To calculate the number of warp ends needed, multiply the *width* of the web on the loom times the *sett.* At each selvedge, the last warp end is usually doubled to add stability to the finished web; this adds another two ends. In Project 3, 13" times 10 e.p.i. equals 130 warp ends, plus two ends for doubled selvedges equals 132 warp ends.

Amount of yarn needed

To calculate the amount of warp yarn needed, multiply the *number of warp ends* times the *length of the warp* on the loom. For Project 3, 132 warp ends times 5 yards length on the loom equals 660 yards needed.

The amount of weft yarn needed varies according to the thickness of the yarn and the type of weaving. A weft-faced weave will require more weft yarn than a warp-faced weave. For the 50/50 weave in Project 3, plan on about the same amount of weft as warp.

Pattern

There are thousands of available weaving patterns and the possibilities for creating your own weaves are endless (see chapter 6, "Recipes for Weaving"). For Project 3, we will set up the loom in a plain tabby weave.

WINDING THE WARP

To measure a number of warp ends and to keep them in order, you will need a *warping board* or a *warp reel.* Reels are usually best for very long warps; in this book we will use warping boards, which are cheap and readily available or can be made from boards and lengths of dowel.

Warp ends are measured on a warping board between pegs, and kept in order by the *cross,* which is the name given to the criss-crossing of warp ends between two close pegs.

To wind the warp, first cut one piece of warp yarn to the correct length. For Project 3, measure a five-yard length. Place it on the warping board,

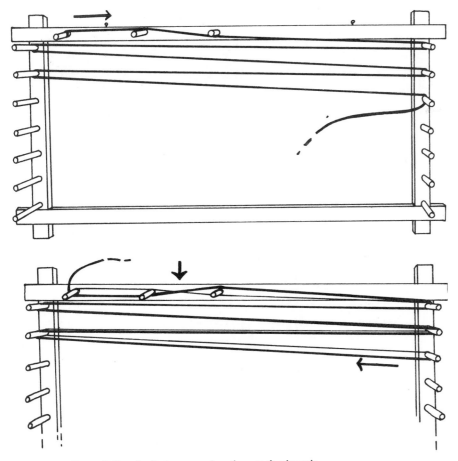

Figure 7.4 *Top,* winding the first warp end on the warping board; *bottom,* the second warp end, showing the cross.

starting at the corner nearest the pegs for the cross and zig-zagging between opposite pegs. The rest of the warp will be wound on the board to the farthest peg reached by this length of yarn.

When winding warp from balls or pull-out skeins, place them in a box on the floor, so they don't bounce all over the room. Cones of yarn can also be put in a box, but it is convenient to have a stand of dowels on a board to support them.

Tie the warp yarn onto the upper peg closest to the cross, and wind on as shown. To count the number of warp ends you have wound, mark every ten ends with a piece of string *at the cross,* as illustrated.

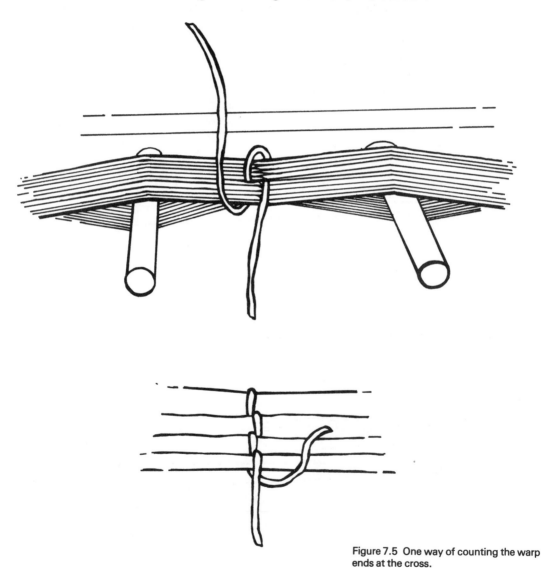

Figure 7.5 One way of counting the warp ends at the cross.

Frequently there are knots in commercial yarns. Since they won't pass through the reed on the loom during weaving, get rid of them while winding the warp. Cut the knot off, tie the end of the yarn to the first or last peg, tie on another yarn, and continue to wind.

Keep the yarn at a steady tension while winding. Yarns with a lot of give can vary greatly in length when stretched unevenly on the board.

To make *vertical* or *warpway stripes* in the finished web, wind different colors of warp on the board. You can plan the width of the stripes by multiplying the width of the finished stripe times the sett; or you can just wind on different colors at random.

Wind the warp, keeping count as shown, stopping when there are the correct number of ends or if it becomes difficult to continue because of the bulk of the warp. For Project 3, we will wind the warp in two smaller sections of 66 ends each.

Now, *tie the cross,* as shown, to keep the ends in order. This is essential in setting up the loom.

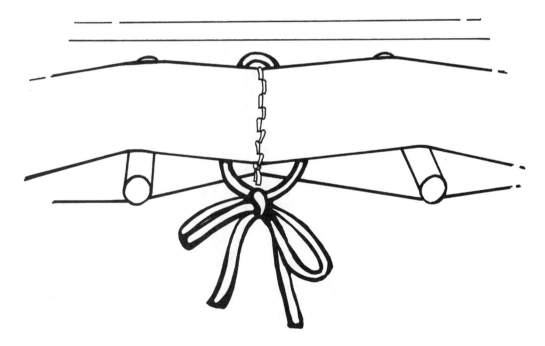

Figure 7.6 Tying the cross.

Tie the warp in a few places to keep it together. Then, remove the warp from the board by hand-chaining as illustrated, keeping it at a tension during the process.

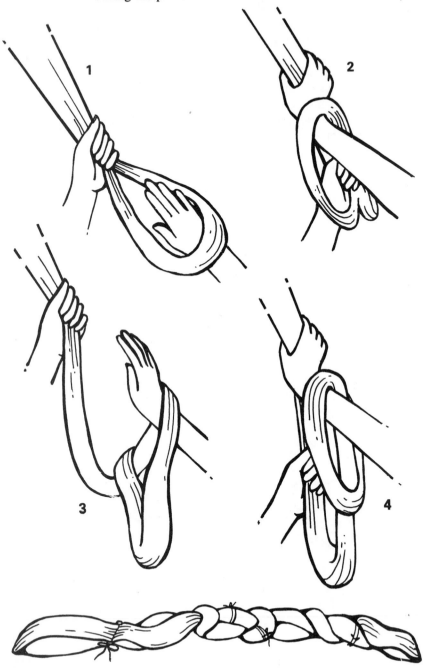

Figure 7.7 Hand-chaining the warp to keep it neat.

116

WARPING THE LOOM

In order to weave, the warp ends must be stretched on the loom in sequence and at an even tension, threaded through the reed and heddles, and rolled neatly on the back beam. There are many ways to set up the loom, which are described in detail in various standard weaving books. Every weaver eventually finds his most comfortable method, the one that is quickest and easiest and produces a nice even warp. Basically, you can set up the loom from the front or the back, with many variations in each of these ways. In this book we will learn one of the quickest methods of warping the loom from the front. For different ways of setting up looms, consult the weaving books listed in chapter 9, "Sources."

SEUCURING THE LEASE STICKS

Insert the thin, strong, flat pieces of wood called *lease sticks* into the open sides of the warp cross. Place them across the breast beam as shown, and tie or tape them with masking tape very securely. Untie the measuring string and that which kept the cross intact.

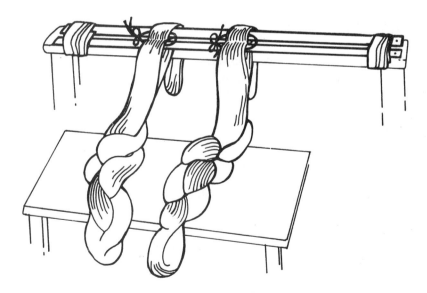

Figure 7.8 Insert the lease sticks through the cross and tie or tape to the breast beam.

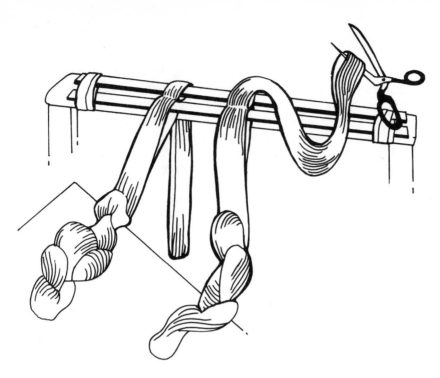

Figure 7.8 (cont'd.) Cutting the warp.

CUTTING THE WARP

Shake out the warp and pull it towards the loom, a small section at a time, until it is long enough to touch the treadles when it hangs down. Then, cut the ends.

SLEYING

First, tie the beater securely between the breast beam and the loom uprights. Measure the reed and mark the middle. Threading the warp through the reed, called *sleying,* starts in the middle and progresses to the right and to the left so you will be sure of having the warp centered on the loom. Divide the chained warp through the middle. In Project 3 there are already two warp chains of equal size. Start with the first warp end on the right and pull it through the reed with a *reed hook.* Thread the next warp end, checking to see that it is the right one (in correct order) at the cross between the lease sticks. Sley the warp according to the correct sett.

118 For Project 3, it is 10 e.p.i. The reed illustrated is a 12-dent reed, with 12

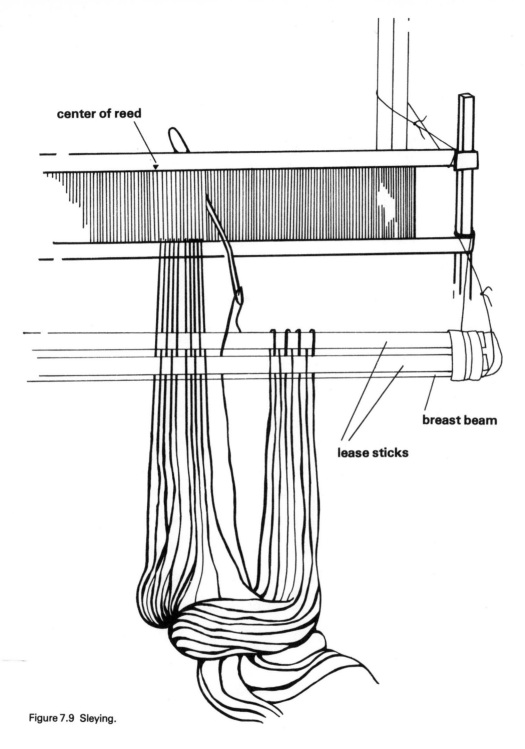

center of reed

breast beam

lease sticks

Figure 7.9 Sleying.

119

spaces per inch; note how it is sleyed: skipping two dents per inch to produce the correct sett. Continue sleying until all the warp has been threaded through the reed. (The last two ends on each selvedge are treated as one warp end; double them and thread through one dent.)

THREADING THROUGH THE HEDDLES

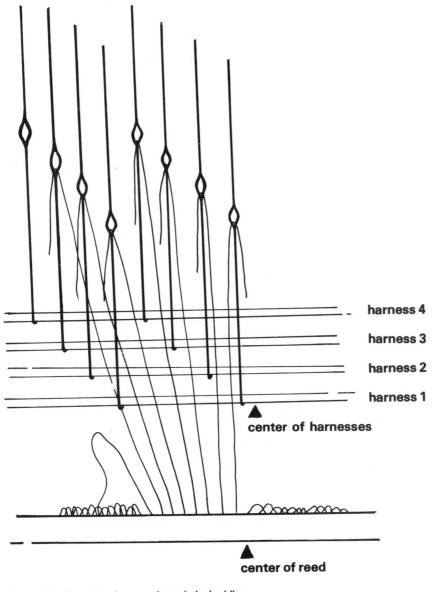

harness 4

harness 3

harness 2

harness 1

center of harnesses

center of reed

Figure 7.10 Threading the warp through the heddles.

The warp ends are threaded through the heddles according to the weaving pattern desired. It is helpful to have a draft for each project at first; after a while you will be able to thread the simpler patterns without a written draft. For Project 3, the pattern is plain or tabby weave. The warp ends will be equally distributed on the four harnesses; make sure that there are enough heddles on each harness for the project.

As with the sleying, start in the middle of the warp and the middle of the harnesses, working towards the right and the left. (Since most drafts are written from right to left, remember to reverse the threading when working from left to right!) For the tabby weave of Project 3, start with the first warp end to the left of center; thread it through the first heddle next to the center in harness 1. Then thread the second warp end through the first heddle next to the center of harness 2, and so on, repeating the process until all the warp ends are threaded. (Treat the doubled selvedge ends as one end.) Check yourself frequently for errors. If the threading is wrong, the weaving will come out incorrectly. Now thread all the ends towards the right, reversing the draft pattern. Start with harness 4, then harness 3, then the second, then the first, and so on until all the ends are threaded. At the back of the harnesses, you can tie the ends loosely in groups as you thread them, to prevent them from coming unthreaded.

TYING ONTO THE BACK APRON

Figure 7.11 The three steps of tying a section of warp to the apron, ending with a half-bow.

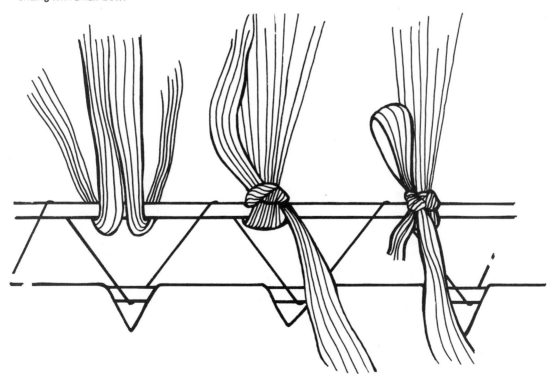

Unroll the back apron from the warp beam and bring it over the back beam until it is 6 inches or so from the heddles. The warp will be tied onto the apron bar in small sections starting from the middle and working out toward both sides. Untie one section of warp ends, and take about 10 or 12 ends for the first knot; tie onto the back bar using the illustrated knot. Tie the rest of the warp to the bar in the same way, taking care to keep the ends an even length.

BEAMING THE LOOM

Figure 7.12 The warp, threaded through the reed and heddles, tied to the back apron, and ready to be beamed.

The warp is now threaded and ready to be rolled onto the warp beam. The mechanism for turning the warp beam varies with different looms check the directions that came with your loom.) It is helpful to have another person help you during this process, although it can be done alone.

One person stands at the front of the loom, shakes the chains of warp to straighten the threads, and holds the warp chains, pulling slightly to keep a good tension while they are being wound on. The other person releases the brake and turns the warp beam slowly by the detachable crank or other mechanism. When there is the *slightest* tangle in the warp or when it pulls at the lease sticks, stop turning the warp beam, shake and

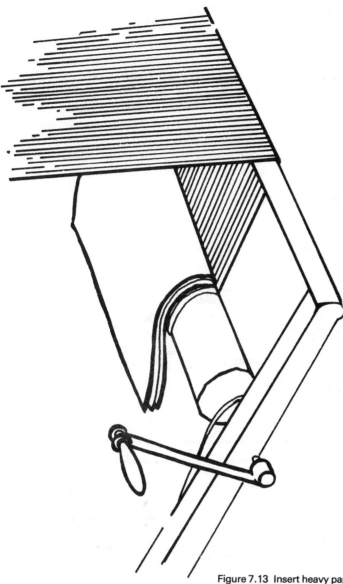

Figure 7.13 Insert heavy papers while rolling the warp onto the warp beam.

pull the warp again to straighten it, and turn the beam again. When the warp has been wound all the way around the beam once, start to pad the warp by winding in heavy paper or several thicknesses of newspaper as you turn the beam. Flat, long sticks called *wind-in sticks* may also be used. Continue to wind the warp on the warp beam in this manner until it comes close to the lease sticks. Then, cut the ends of the warp, remove the lease sticks from the loom, and wind the warp to within a few inches of the front of the reed.

123

TYING ONTO THE FRONT APRON

Bring the front apron around and over the breast beam. The warp will be tied in the same way as it was on the back apron, with one exception. Tie the knots as before, from the center of the warp and towards the sides, but don't tie the half-bow as before. When all the sections have been tied, test the warp for tension by pressing your hand across the warp stretched towards the reed. It is very important for the warp to have the same tension or springiness across the width of the web. Tighten looser sections and test again. When you are satisfied with the even tension, tie half-bows on all the sections. The loom is now ready for weaving!

FILLING THE SHUTTLES

There are many different kinds of shuttles for weaving, some specifically designed for certain forms of weaving. A tiny tapestry shuttle would be un-

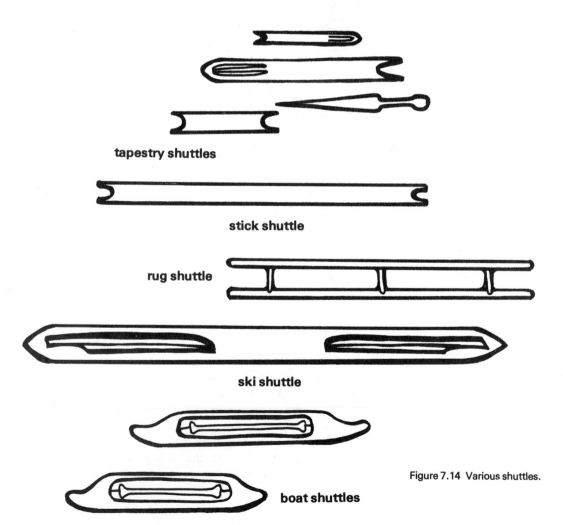

tapestry shuttles

stick shuttle

rug shuttle

ski shuttle

Figure 7.14 Various shuttles.

boat shuttles

suitable for weaving rugs, and boat shuttles would be inconvenient for use in tapestries. A good, many-purpose shuttle is the *ski shuttle,* as it holds a great deal of yarn at once and slides easily through the shed. Most weavers start out with a few *boat shuttles,* as they are particularly useful for small projects and finer yarns.

Ski shuttles and tapestry shuttles can be filled by simply winding on the yarn; boat shuttles and many other shuttles contain bobbins of wound yarn. To wind the yarn on a bobbin, place the bobbin on a *bobbin winder* (which

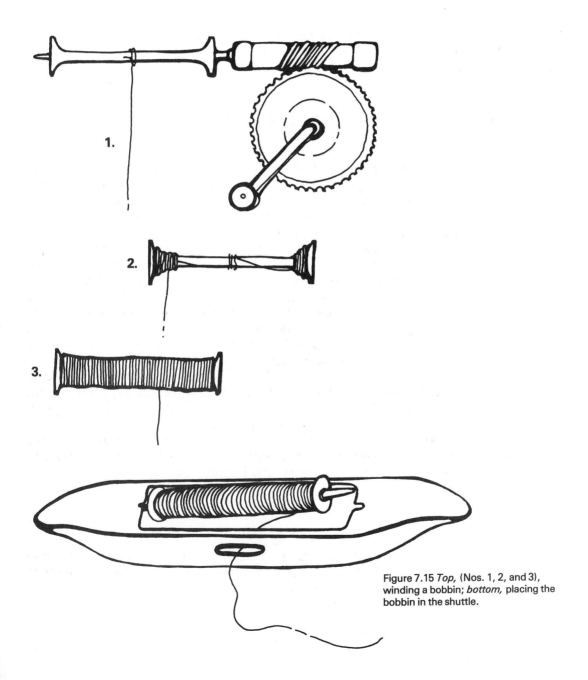

1.

2.

3.

Figure 7.15 *Top,* (Nos. 1, 2, and 3), winding a bobbin; *bottom,* placing the bobbin in the shuttle.

clamps onto a table or shelf) and wind the yarn a few times around the center of the bobbin until it holds. Then wind the yarn around one end, then the other, as shown. The rest of the yarn is wound back and forth on the central portion of the bobbin. Don't wind the yarn any thicker than the edge of the bobbin. You might find it helpful to wind several bobbins of the same color at once. Then, place the bobbin in the shuttle as shown.

THE TIE-UP

Tie the treadles to the lams according to the pattern draft you are using (see chapter 6). For the next four project outlined in this book, use a *direct tie-up*.

WEAVING THE HEADING

The first pick or so of weaving, called the *heading,* is useful for testing the accuracy of the threading and the tie-up. To weave the heading, use a heavier yarn. Adjust the tension of the warp by the handle that turns the cloth beam, releasing the brake at the same time. The warp should be taut, but not so stretched that it snaps easily.

Step on treadle *a,* which raises harnesses 1 and 3; slide the shuttle through the shed, from right to left and close to the reed. If you are using a boat shuttle, have the long flat side against the reed. Turn the yarn end around the outside warp end and back into the shed. Release the treadle, hold the beater in the center, and pull it towards you firmly. Step on treadle *b,* raising harnesses 2 and 4, "throw" the shuttle as before, release the treadle, and beat. Repeat these two *picks,* or rows, a few more times, then check the heading carefully for errors.

For *threading errors,* untie the section with the error from the front apron, rethread the ends correctly, and retie. If the weaving is not straight across the web, the warp has been tied onto the apron at an *uneven tension.* Untie the looser sections and retie them.

When all mistakes have been corrected, end the heading by turning the last weft pick around the outer warp end and back into the shed; then cut. *This is the way all weft is begun and ended.*

WEAVING

The beauty of the process of weaving is its rhythm. Every weaver's rhythm is different for the three basic steps in weaving: treadling, throwing the shuttle, and beating.

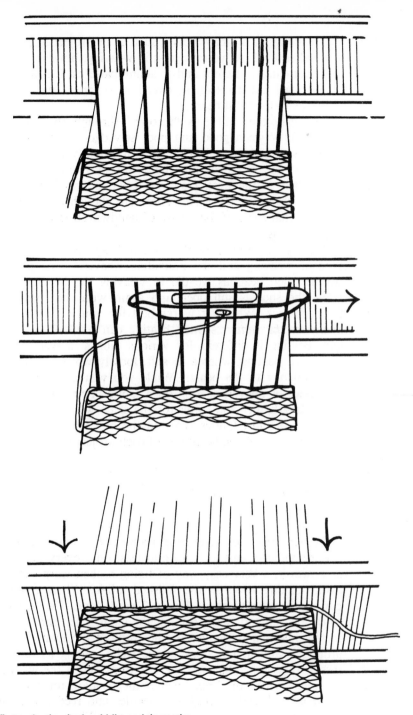

Figure 7.16 *Top,* first make the shed; *middle,* and throw the
shuttle; *bottom,* then beat.

127

Treadling for a tabby weave, such as in Project 3, is the simplest; *a* and *b* are alternated. As you progress in weaving, however, you might run into more complicated tie-ups and treadling patterns. It is helpful when weaving an involved pattern such as overshot to tape a paper with the treadling sequence to the front beam.

The way the shuttle is "thrown" through the open shed makes the difference between good and poor selvedges. Watch for pulling-in of the selvedges caused by pulling the yarn too tightly when throwing the shuttle. Loops at the selvedges are the result of overcompensation—letting too much slack in the weft. Don't be a perfectionist, though, especially when you are beginning to weave. There are enough things to think about! Remember that some of the charm of handwoven things comes from the little imperfections.

Methods of beating of the weft pick against the woven web vary with type of weaving and the individual weaver. Some prefer to release the treadle, then beat, as we did in weaving the heading. Others beat once while the shed is still open and again with the shed closed—two beats for each pick. Whatever works best for you is fine. *Be sure to hold the beater in the center;* slanted beating can result from holding it at either end. Beating is different for various fabrics; a weft-faced tapestry needs very hard beating, whereas a soft, loosely woven baby blanket requires a light touch with the beater. While you weave you will become aware of the effect of uneven beating on a fabric. You can create specialty fabrics by beating harder and softer for the same web, but it doesn't help the appearance of most fabrics. To find the best way of beating, try a few different methods at the beginning of each project.

BROKEN WARP ENDS

Perhaps the most agonizing problem for a weaver is the snapping of a warp end; it seems to happen at least once every time you weave. There is, however, a very easy way of fixing broken warp ends. The object is to avoid making knots in the finished fabric. When a warp thread breaks, cut another thread about 1½ to 2 yards long. Tie it, with a square knot, to the broken end at the *back* of the loom. Then thread it through the correct heddle and reed towards the front of the loom. Wind it around and around a straight pin stuck in the web, keeping its tension similar to the rest of the warp. That's all there is to it. When the warp has advanced to the point where the knot reaches the heddles, untie the knot, thread the original warp end through the heddles and reed toward the front of the looms, and wind it around another pin. When the web is taken off the loom, the ends can be woven into the web with a needle or crochet hook, then snipped off.

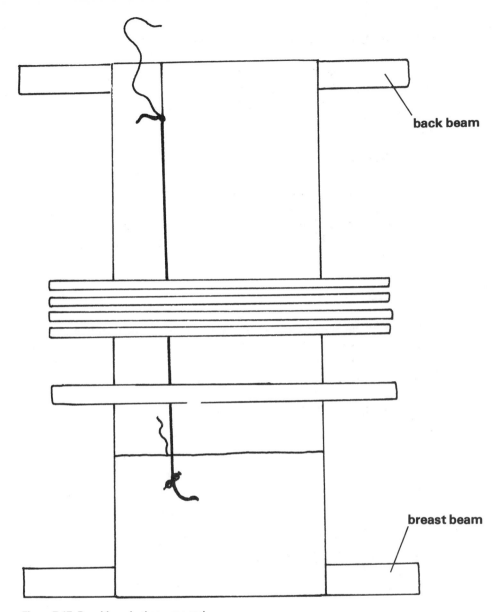

back beam

breast beam

Figure 7.17 Repairing a broken warp end.

WEAVING AND ADVANCING THE WARP

Most weavers agree that you should weave weft onto only a few inches of the warp at a time. The web is then advanced a few inches more by releasing the foot brake and winding the web onto the cloth beam with the handle mechanism. If you advance the warp too far, beating will become **129** awkward and uneven and even the appearance of the web can change.

MEASURING THE WEB AS YOU WEAVE

Usually you need to know how much you have woven, whether for weaving a pattern or for weaving a number of articles on the same web. One way to measure the web is to pin a tape measure to the edge, adding pins as you weave more (and adding measuring tapes as you need them!).

REMOVING THE WEB

When you have finished weaving the proper length (don't forget to add the allowance for "take-up"), the web is ready to be taken from the loom. Untie the half-bows from the back apron, and pull the warp to the front of the loom. Unwind the web from the front apron, and untie the front knots.

FINISHING

Weave all broken ends into the web about an inch with a needle or crochet hook. Cut closely all weft yarn at the beginnings and endings of colors and bobbins. You might want to steam-press the web at this point. Finish each project according to the directions given.

TYING NEW ENDS ONTO AN OLD WARP

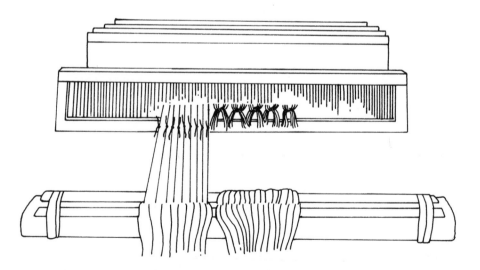

Figure 7.18 Setting up the loom by tying new warp onto old warp ends.

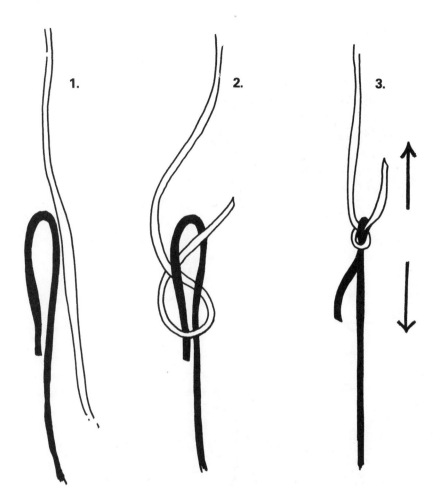

Figure 7.18 (cont'd.) Using the weaver's knot.

When your next project will have the *same number of warp ends* and the *same threading* as the one you are taking off the loom, you might want to save yourself some time by tying the new warp ends onto the old ones. When you are finished with the present weaving, cut the warp ends a few inches *in front of* the reed, and tie loosely in sections. Set up the new warp as before, with the lease sticks on the front beam, and cut the new warp ends. Then, tie each new warp end to an old one, using the *weaver's knot* as shown, and keeping them in order. When all the knots have been tied, pull the warp ends, a few at a time, through the reed and heddles. Then you are ready to roll the warp onto the warp beam as before.

131

PROJECT 3— PLACE MATS

threading draft

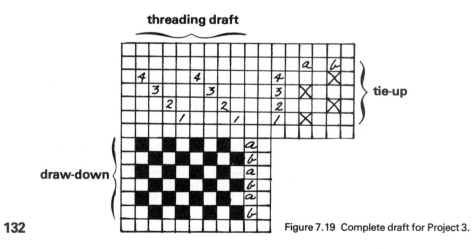

tie-up

draw-down

Figure 7.19 Complete draft for Project 3.

ARTICLE. Six place mats.

PATTERN. Tabby, 50/50.

SIZE. *Finished size*—12" by 18" with ½" fringe at each end, or 12" by 19." Total for 6 mats is 12" by 114." *On the loom*—13" by 5 yards.

WARP. Strong, medium-weight yarn such as cotton, wool, linen, or synthetic. In the illustrated sample, rust and gold synthetic yarn was used.

WEFT. Same weight yarn as the warp. In the sample, rust, gold, and brown synthetic yarn was used.

SETT. 10 e.p.i. In a 12-dent reed, the warp is sleyed as follows: five, space, five, space, etc.

NUMBER OF WARP ENDS NEEDED. 132 warp ends (including double selvedges) or 130 *working* warp ends.

AMOUNT OF YARN NEEDED. About 660 yards of each warp and weft.

WEAVING. Follow the general instructions for winding the warp and setting up the loom. If you want, wind the warp in different colors to produce warp stripes, as in the sample. While weaving, pay special attention to the selvedges and to the evenness of the beating. Weft stripes can be woven at random, as shown in the sample.

FINISHING: Weave in all broken ends, and cut all ends of yarn where a color or new bobbin began or ended. Cut 19" lengths from the web for the six place mats. Unravel ½" at each end of each mat, and finish with a *whip stitch,* as shown in figure 00.0, using a yarn needle and weft yarn; or finish with a *zig-zag stitch* on your sewing machine.

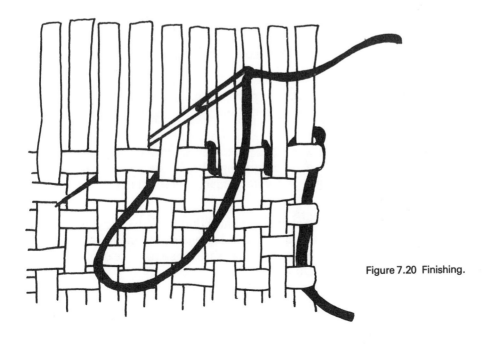

Figure 7.20 Finishing.

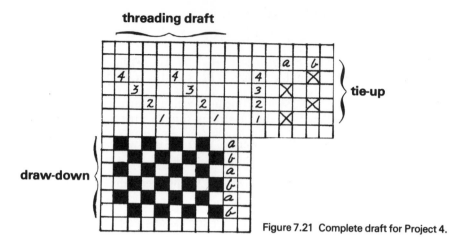

Figure 7.21 Complete draft for Project 4.

PROJECT 4—WALL HANGING

ARTICLE. One wall hanging.

PATTERN. Tabby, weft-faced, with tapestry techniques.

SIZE. *Finished*—12" by 12" or 12" by 18." *On the loom*—13" by 3 yards.

WARP. Very strong, medium-weight yarn such as linen, jute, or similar synthetic.

WEFT. Medium-to-heavy yarns; wool, cotton, synthetics; handspun wool is ideal. Select your colors with care.

SETT. 6 e.p.i. In a 12-dent reed, use alternate sley.

NUMBER OF WARP ENDS NEEDED: 90 (including double selvedges) or 88 working warp ends.

AMOUNT OF YARN NEEDED. For the warp, 270 yards. For the weft, the amount will vary according to the size of the yarn and the closeness of beating.

WEAVING. Follow the general instructions for winding the warp and setting up the loom. Weave a heading. Weave the hanging, using one or more of the following tapestry techniques. Finish the web with an inch or so of plain weave.

FINISHING. Tie fringes at the top and bottom of the hanging, using the method used in Projects 1 and 2 or using one of the methods shown. You may add macramé knotting or tie on shells, beads, or feathers. Hang the weaving from a stick or dowel.

134

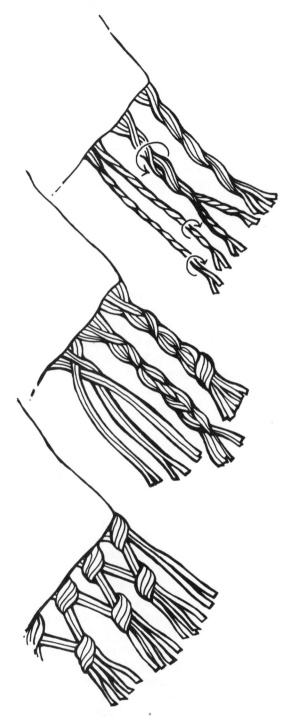

Figure 7.22 Other fringes: *top,* double knot; *middle,* braided; *bottom,* twisted.

135

Weaving a tapestry can be a very creative experience. To encourage your originality, I have given no precise instructions for the design of the wall hanging. We will look at three tapestry techniques that have been used throughout history and that are still extremely popular. Try to plan a design that will incorporate all of these techniques in one hanging. If you like, draw a diagram or "cartoon" of the design before weaving and refer to it during weaving. You might, however, prefer to plan the wall hanging while you weave it.

Although many meanings have been given for the term *tapestry,* including intricate medieval embroideries, we will use the modern weaver's definition. In this context, tapestry is handwoven, weft-faced fabric, its pattern determined by finger-manipulated techniques.

Tapestries are often woven on frame looms or on special tapestry looms. There are special bobbins, shuttles, and beaters available that are well worth buying if you plan to do a lot of tapestry weaving. For an occasional tapestry, though, use your frame loom or floor loom, hand butterflies, and either the loom beater or a table fork for beating.

SOUMAK

There are countless variations of this ancient decorative technique. In soumak, a weft yarn is wound around the warp in a particular way to form ridges or bands of color. There are vertical and slanting soumak techniques as well as the horizontal ones shown. To give stability to the fabric with soumak, other weft yarn is woven in the tabby weave at intervals between picks of soumak.

To begin a soumak pick, make a shed and begin a contrasting yarn as usual, tucking the yarn around the selvedge end and into the shed. Release the shed. Lifting the appropriate warp ends with your fingers, wind the yarn around the warp in one of the ways illustrated. On the next pick, the soumak may be slanted in either the same or opposite direction. Experiment (even while weaving the hanging!) with the single and double soumak shown here, and note the differing characteristics given to the fabric. In between every pick, or every few picks of soumak, weave two picks of

tabby weave with the background color.

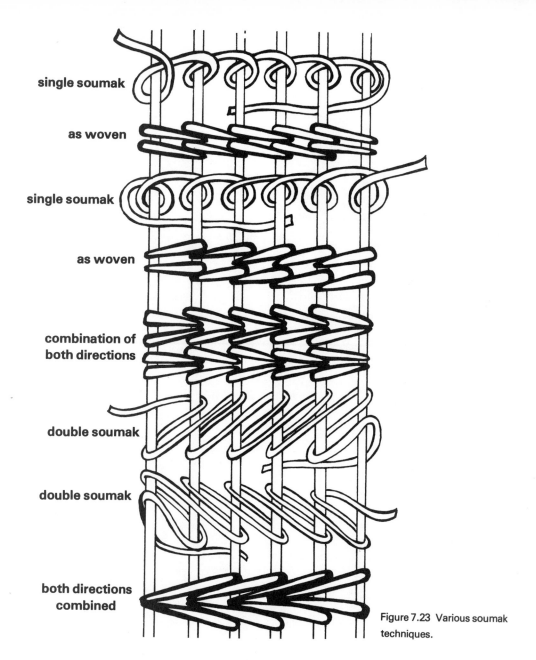

single soumak

as woven

single soumak

as woven

combination of
both directions

double soumak

double soumak

both directions
combined

Figure 7.23 Various soumak
techniques.

SLITS

Slits in a tapestry web, formed at the boundaries of pattern areas, are a characteristic of Polish *kilim* tapestries. They can be sewn together after the web is removed from the loom, or left alone. One of the easiest tapestry **137** techniques, they can make delightful borders, as illustrated.

Figure 7.24 Slit tapestry technique.

To make slits, you will need as many different shuttles or butterflies as you have pattern areas or colors. Make a shed, and begin the first separate weft yarn as usual. Pass it through the shed *only* as far as the end of the first area you have planned; then begin the next color. Repeat across the first pick, for as many different slits as you want. For the second pick, make the alternate shed and pass each color through the shed, again only as far as the pattern areas. Repeat these picks until the slits are as long as you want them. For diagonally slanted areas, use the same technique, except "moving over" one or two warp ends in each pick, depending upon the amount of slant desired.

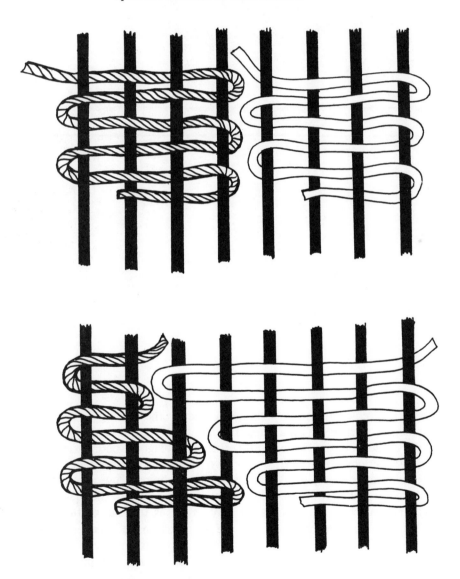

Figure 7.25 *Top,* vertical slit technique; *bottom,* diagonal slit technique.

Figure 7.26 An example of interlocking weft techniques.

Pattern or color areas may also be formed by the turning of weft yarns around each other in the same shed. If done with care, this technique makes the web completely reversible. Both vertical and diagonal boundaries can be made by interlocking the weft one or two warps further in either direction with each subsequent pick. When using this technique, use a butterfly or shuttle for each color or pattern area. Make the shed, begin the first color as usual, and pass it through the shed only as far as the end of the pattern area. Repeat this with each color. On the next pick, make the alternate shed and interlock the colors as shown, taking care to make the twist in the *center* of the warp ends. Repeat these two picks until the pattern areas are completed.

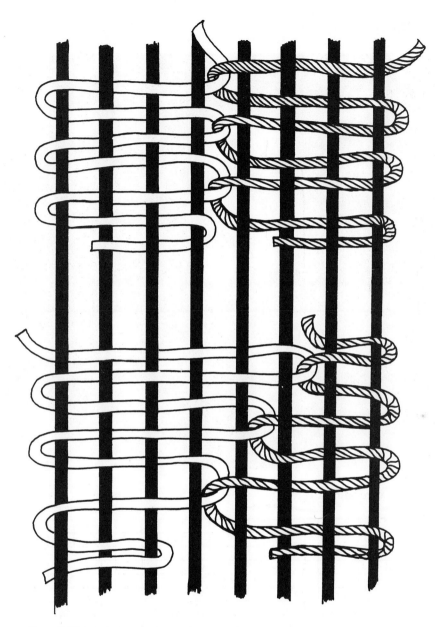

Figure 7.27 Interlocking weft technique; *top,* vertical; *bottom,* diagonal.

GHIORDES KNOT

You might also want to incorporate the Ghiordes knot, as learned in chapter 5, in this wall hanging.

141

PROJECT 5—ONE SCARF

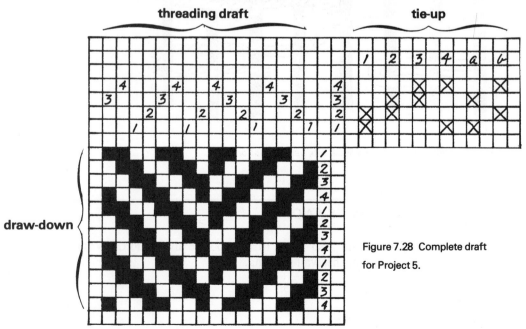

draw-down

Figure 7.28 Complete draft for Project 5.

ARTICLE. One scarf.

PATTERN. Twill, broken; *dornik,* 50/50.

SIZE. *Finished*—12" by 54" *On the loom*—13" by 3 yards.

WARP. Medium to light-weight wool or synthetic. In the illustrated sample, a combination yarn (75 percent wool and 25 percent rayon) was used; the colors were wine, brown, and taupe.

WEFT. Same as warp.

SETT. 10 e.p.i. In a 12-dent reed, the warp is sleyed five, space, five, space, etc.

NUMBER OF WARP ENDS NEEDED. 132 warp ends (including double selvedges) or 130 working ends.

AMOUNT OF YARN NEEDED. About 400 yards for each warp and weft.

WEAVING. Follow the general instructions for winding the warp and setting up the loom. The warp can be wound on the board in different colors to produce vertical stripes. You can also weave different colors in the weft to produce horizonal stripes.

FINISHING. Weave in all broken ends; cut off all dangling ends as usual; finish with a short fringe, either knotted or sewn with a whip stitch as in Project 3.

PROJECT 6—BABY BLANKET OR THROW BLANKET

ARTICLE. One baby blanket or throw blanket.

PATTERN. Twill, bird's eye, 50/50.

SIZE. *Finished*—40" by 54," plus a 2" fringe at both ends, or 40" by 58." *On the loom*—42" by 4 yards.

WARP. Synthetic sport yarn, or medium-weight wool (for a baby blanket use the synthetic). In the illustrated sample, red, white and blue "supermarket" acrylic was used for both warp and weft.

WEFT. Same as warp; or, for throw blanket, you could use wool or mohair for contrast.

SETT. 8 e.p.i. In a 12-dent reed, sley as follows: two, space, two, space, etc.

NUMBER OF WARP ENDS NEEDED. 338 warp ends (including double selvedges) or 336 working ends.

AMOUNT OF YARN NEEDED. About 1400 yards of warp, and about the same amount for the weft.

Figure 7.29 (Photo by Chris Alderman.)

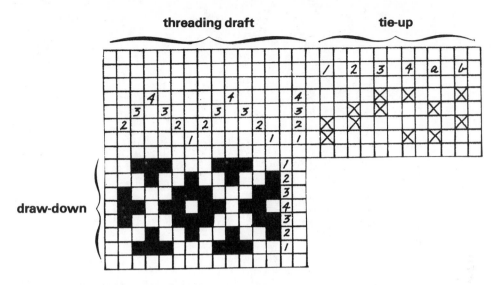

Figure 7.30 Complete draft for Project 6.

WEAVING. Follow the general instructions for winding the warp, setting up the loom, and weaving. In the sample shown, vertical stripes were made by winding different colored yarn on the warping board; horizontal stripes by different colors in the weft.

FINISHING. Use a 2" fringe, knotting as in Projects 1 and 2.

PROJECT 7—TABLE RUNNER

ARTICLE. One table runner.

PATTERN. Overshot, *pine bloom 50/50.*

SIZE. *Finished*—about 12" by 36," with 1½" fringe at both ends. *On the loom*—13" by 5 yards.

WARP. 8/2 or 8/3 cotton, linen, or synthetic.

WEFT. Tabby—8/2 cotton, linen, or synthetic. Pattern—medium 2-ply wool or synthetic.

SETT. 12 e.p.i. In a 12-dent reed, sley singly.

NUMBER OF WARP ENDS NEEDED. 161 warp ends (including double selvedges) or 159 working ends. There are three repeats of the pattern.

AMOUNT OF YARN NEEDED. About 800 yards of warp and tabby; about 800 yards of pattern.

145

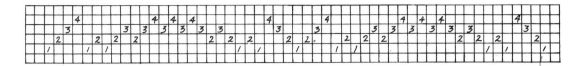

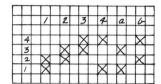

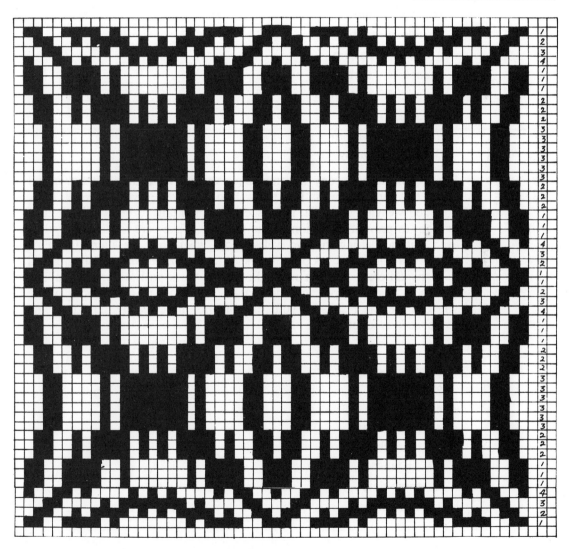

Figure 7.31 Complete draft for Project 7. *Top,* threading draft;
middle, tie-up; *bottom,* draw-down.

WEAVING. Follow the general instructions for winding the warp, setting up the loom, and weaving the heading. While threading the warp through the heddles, check frequently for accuracy. The sample shown makes use of vertical stripes made by winding different colored warp on the warping board.

We have seen (in chapter 6) that in weaving overshot patterns, two weft shuttles are used—the tabby thread and the pattern thread. The draw-down and treadling sequence given refer to the pattern thread. The tabby thread is treadled *a,b,a,b, between* the pattern picks. To weave the beginning of the pattern, use the following treadling sequence:

Treadle 1—pattern
Treadle *a*—tabby
Treadle 2—pattern
Treadle *b*—tabby
Treadle 3—pattern
Treadle *a*—tabby
Treadle 4—pattern
Treadle *b*—tabby

It is a good idea to copy the treadling sequence from the draw-down and tape it to your loom or pin it to the web to guide you as you weave.

When weaving overshot, it is especially important to beat with an even tension, to prevent distortion in the patterns. Take care to keep the edges even, without letting the two wefts "loop" when they are alternated. Pine bloom is a particularly popular overshot, as it can be successfully treadled in many different ways. You might like to work with different treadling sequences, first on paper, in various draw-downs, or first at the loom, where you can see the results of your experiments more readily. The treadling sequence is as follows:

1
2
3
4
1—three times
2—three times
3—six times
2—three times
1—three times
4
3
2
1

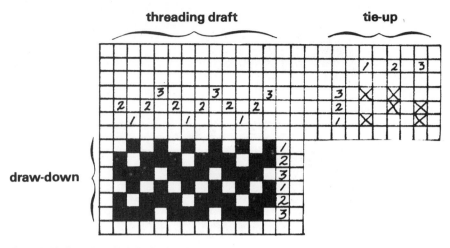

Figure 7.32 Complete draft for Project 8.

PROJECT 8—WALL HANGING

ARTICLE. One wall hanging.

PATTERN. Three-harness *krokbragd,* weft-faced.

SIZE. *Finished*—14" by 36" (with long fringe at both ends.) *On the loom—* 15" by 5 yards.

WARP. Medium-weight linen, jute, or similar synthetic.

WEFT. Medium-weight one- or two-ply wool or synthetic.

SETT. 5 or 6 e.p.i. In a 12-dent reed; use alternate sley.

NUMBER OF WARP ENDS NEEDED. 86 warp ends, (including double selvedges) or 84 working ends.

AMOUNT OF YARN NEEDED. 430 yards of warp; amount of weft varies according to size and beating.

WEAVING. Follow the general instructions for winding the warp, setting up the loom, and weaving the heading. The three-harness *krokbragd* is a Norwegian weave that looks much like a finger-manipulated tapestry weave. It is loom-controlled, however, which makes it much quicker to weave, and its construction makes it ideal for heavy fabrics used in wall hangings, pillow covers, and rugs. The striking appearance of the three-harness *krokbragd,* moreover, adds to its popularity and versatility.

149

Figure 7.33 Pillows woven in three-harness *krokbragd,* a Norwegian technique.

The only disadvantage of this weave is that it cannot be done very well on a counter-balanced loom, as it is an unbalanced weave (note the treadling sequence and tie-up). In the construction of the *krokbragd,* the first pick (which is in tabby weave) is completely hidden by the "floats" formed by the other two picks. This gives added strength and thickness to the finished web.

The sequence of treadling never varies: 1,2,3,1,2,3. The pattern is formed by the sequence of the colors used. The maximum number of weft colors used in one pattern sequence is three; any number of colors can be used in the entire web. It is traditional to carry one color from one sequence into the next. For instance, here is a typical color sequence (remember that the treadling sequence never changes):

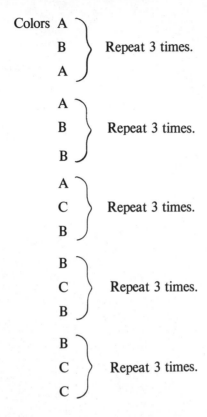

Colors A
        B   } Repeat 3 times.
        A

        A
        B   } Repeat 3 times.
        B

        A
        C   } Repeat 3 times.
        B

        B
        C   } Repeat 3 times.
        B

        B
        C   } Repeat 3 times.
        C

Experiment with colors with this weave, and you will be delighted with the results.

8 To Market, To Market!

ADVANTAGES OF SELLING HANDCRAFTS

From the moment you first become involved in spinning, dyeing, and weaving, you'll find that your friends will be begging to buy some of your handspun yarn or original weavings. And before too long, when you start to calculate the considerable investment you are making in materials, selling your spinning and weaving for a profit will seem like a very good idea! But, like any business venture, selling handcrafts can be a tremendous success or a real headache—and it is usually a combination of the two!

SATISFACTION

The first time that someone pays hard cash for a basket of your hand-dyed homespun yarn or a handwoven wall hanging is very exciting. All the thought and time that went into the creation of your handmade goods seems worthwhile. For another person to admire your work so much that they *pay* for it is encouraging and flattering. And it is a very good feeling to

153

know that you have designed and fashioned something that will be appreciated and loved. It gives a craftsperson great confidence to sell weavings and spinnings. And with self-confidence comes the ability to stretch your mind and to think even more imaginatively.

FAME

No matter how you decide to sell your crafts (and you will probably attempt several ways before finding your favorite), you will come into contact with other weavers, spinners, and dyers. It is fun to exchange ideas, weaving patterns, and sources for yarns and materials; and it can be very stimulaing to get to know the distinct individualities of other craftspeople and their products. And other spinners and weavers will be just as anxious to know *you*. It is surprising how quickly word gets around about new people in the business. Your own style of spinning or weaving will become your trademark, and soon you may even be approached with special orders and commissions!

FORTUNE

The more dubious advantage of selling crafts seems to be money! To be able to sell your products at reasonable prices while still using good-quality materials leaves very little money left over to pay for your *time*. And, as you know, the arts of dyeing, spinning and weaving are time-consuming. Briefly, if you have lots of time, and don't expect to get an hourly wage out of it, selling crafts may be for you.

There is something nice, though, about generating enough money from your crafts to pay for your materials and equipment. And, when you are spinning and weaving items to be sold, your loom and wheel are always in use. The more experience you get, the better you will become.

DISADVANTAGES OF SELLING HANDCRAFTS

TIME

The first thing you will notice about selling your goods is that it can be extremely time-consuming. Many hours are spent going from door-to-door, meeting with advertisers, or sitting at a craft fair booth. Whatever type of selling you choose, you will probably come to resent all the driving, bargaining, and bookkeeping that is a large part of the selling process. Time spent in selling is time away from the loom and the wheel.

CREATIVITY

When you start to sell more than an occasional ball of yarn or woven pillow, you will soon realize that you just can't get very far (if making money is your objective) with one-of-a-kind items. You will probably settle on one or a few salable items to make and sell. And no matter how creative you are, it is easy to get bogged down when you mass-produce your crafts. "Cranking out" twenty handwoven blankets for a wholesale order might be great for the pocketbook, but it doesn't do much for your morale. For some people, the "conveyer-belt syndrome" can take a lot of the joy out of creating.

PROFIT

If you are selling your crafts as a hobby, the obstacles to making a worthwhile profit won't concern you. However, you might want to make a living from it, or at least a healthy supplemental income. And it is not impossible. We all know of people who have made a financial success of making and selling crafts. With careful planning and some old-fashioned common sense, you can have a very fulfilling vocation.

PLANNING YOUR SELLING

THE LEGAL ANGLE

The first step in selling of any kind is to find out about your federal, state, and local laws. There are tax laws, laws for small businesses, and even zoning laws that can be of prime importance to you. Even if you only plan to sell a few items a year, you might be required to pay a dollar or two for a special license in your state; some states issue licenses, for example, for such things as stuffing pillows or toys. There are reasons, however obscure, for all of these regulations; and we all know how inconvenient it can be to pay a fine for inadvertently breaking a rule. It is worth it to do a little research at your local city hall!

EVALUATING YOUR MARKET

One secret of a good small business is careful planning. Before settling on one type of selling, find out about the *competition* you will be facing; the *number* and *type* of people who are likely to buy your goods; *what* they prefer to buy; and the kind of *resources* you should have to be successful in your particular area.

The local Small Business Administration can be very helpful in answering general and specific questions about starting a business and about local possibilities. But the best way to determine what kind of market you can expect is to scout around yourself, talking to as many people as you can. Shopkeepers of craft stores, local craftspeople, small merchants, local bankers and government officials, and your friends and neighbors can all contribute valid information.

TYPES OF MARKETING

You will probably find the best method for selling your products by experimentation. The first one most craftspeople try is selling articles to *stores for resale.* The shopkeeper will either buy your handcrafts *outright* or will take them on *consignment.* When he pays you cash for your goods, you will probably receive a bit less money; but there is the advantage of having made a final sale of your goods. When the shopkeeper takes your things on consignment, on the other hand, you will not get any money until they have been sold in the store. You might get paid slightly more than than when you sell outright, but if the goods are not sold in a few months, the shopkeeper will return them to you, usually somewhat shopworn. The percentage of profit in selling to stores varies; but a common one is 40 percent of the selling price for the store and 60 percent for the craftsperson.

Another very popular way to sell crafts is at **fairs.** State or county fairs, and the increasingly numerous crafts fairs will welcome craftspeople with an ample supply of saleable items of good quality. You will probably have to pay for running a booth and you might have to provide display tables. If you are a member of a spinning or weaving guild or society, the entrance fee, the work of setting up the booth, and the actual process of selling, can be split among the participants. Many people have had great success in fairs, especially when large suppliers come to examine their wares and place wholesale orders for the coming year. It is possible, with just the right combination of energy, talent, sales ability, and luck to make a fine living from your crafts at fairs alone. There have been, though, financial failures at this type of selling. And many artists resent the ignorance and lack of appreciation they often encounter at fairs; this, of course, depends on the kind of fair, the area, and the crowd itself.

Owning your own shop is, for some, the most satisfying way to sell crafts. Probably the greatest requirements are ample time, energy, and capital. You could have just a summer store, or work out of your own home. You should, of course, be prepared for both the built-in joys and hassles of owning your own business.

Some folks find that the most practical combination of selling methods is the *crafts cooperative,* in which several people pool together their money, time, and talent. The key to such an enterprise is in the name, and cooperation between members can be encouraged by careful planning and flexible rules.

Perhaps selling your crafts in any of these ways will be rewarding to you, but it's possible that your greatest satisfaction will always be found in the actual processes: spinning the raw wool into lovely yarn, dyeing the skeins unique colors, and creating your own beautiful and functional weavings.

9 Sources

YARNS, FIBERS, FLEECES, SPINNING WHEELS AND SUPPLIES, LOOMS AND WEAVING SUPPLIES, AND DYEING SUPPLIES

Black Sheep Weaving and Craft Supply
318 sw 2nd Street
Corvallis, Oregon 97330

Colonial Textiles
82 Plants Dam Road
East Lyme, Conn. 06333

Earth Guild/Grateful Union
149 Putnan Avenue
Cambridge, Mass. 02139

Robin and Russ Handweavers
533 Adams Street
McMinnville, Oregon 97128

Straw Into Gold
P.O. Box 2904
Oakland, Calif. 94618

159

YARNS AND FIBERS

Briggs & Little's Woolen Mill Ltd.
York Mills, N.B., Canada

Christopher Farm
R.F.D. 2
Richmond, Maine 04357

Condon's Yarns
Wm. Condon & Sons Ltd.
P.O. Box 129
Charlottetown, P.E.I., Canada

Contessa Yarns
P.O. Box 37
Lebanon, Conn. 06249

Craft Yarns of Rhode Island, Inc.
Main St.
P.O. Box 151
Harrisville, Rhode Island 02830

Creative Handweavers
P.O. Box 26480
Los Angeles, Calif. 90026

Fort Crailo Yarns Company
2 Green Street
Rensselaer, N.Y. 12144

Frankemuth Woolen Mill Co.
570 South Main
Frankemuth, Mich. 48734

Frederick J. Fawcett Inc.
129 South Street
Boston, Mass. 02111

The H. H. Perkins Company
10 South Bradley Road
Woodbridge, Conn. 06525

House of Yarns and Fabrics
P.O. Box 98
Hampton, New Hampshire 13842

Lily Mills Company
Shelby, North Carolina 28150

Mary A. Chase
Brooksville, Maine 04617

Shuttlecraft
P.O. Box 6041
Providence 4, Rhode Island 02904

Stanley-Berroco, Inc.
Mendon Street
Uxbridge, Mass. 01569

Tahki Imports Ltd.
336 West End Avenue
New York, N.Y. 10023

Terlingua Designs
4120 Rio Bravo
El Paso, Texas 79902

The Weaver's Store
875 Auburn St.
Auburndale, Mass. 02166

Yarn Primitives
P.O. Box 1013
Weston, Conn. 06880

LOOMS AND WEAVING SUPPLIES

Gilmore Looms/E. E. Gilmore
1032 North Broadway
Stockton, Cal. 95205

Nilus Leclerc Inc.
L'Isletville, Quebec, Canada

Leclerc Corp.
P.O. Box 491
Plattsburg, N.Y. 12901

Leclerc West Dist.
P.O. Box 7012
Landscape Station
Berkeley, Calif. 94707

Lorellyn Looms
Chicago Park, Calif. 95712

L. W. Macomber Co.
166 Essex Street
Saugus, Mass.

BOOKS

Your Handspinning. Elsie Davenport. Craft and Hobby
  Book Service, Pacific Grove, Calif.
Dye Plants and Dyeing. Brooklyn Botanic Garden, Brooklyn, N.Y.
Natural Dyes and Home Dyeing. Rita J. Adrosko.
  Dover Publications, Inc., New York.
The New Key to Weaving. Mary E. Black. The Bruce
  Publishing Company, New York.
Shuttle-craft Book of American Handweaving. Mary M.
  Atwater. The Macmillan Company, New York.

CATALOG OF BOOKS

Craft and Hobby Book Service
P.O. Box 626
Pacific Grove, Calif. 93850

MAGAZINES

Craft Horizons
44 West 53rd Street
New York, N.Y. 10019

Shuttle, Spindle, and Dyepot
998 Farmington Avenue
West Hartford, Conn. 06107

The Shuttle Craft Guild
4499 Delta River Rd., Rt. 1
Lansing, Michigan 48906

161

Index

A

Afghans, 90
Alpaca, 14, 22
Acrylic yarn, 17
Angora, 14
Animal fibers, 7, 13-14; in spinning, 22
    alpaca, 14, 22
    angora, 14
    camel hair, 14, 22
    cashmere, 14, 22
    cow hair, 22
    dog hair, 22
    fleece, 24
    goat hair, 14, 22
    human hair, 22
    llama hair, 14
    mohair, 14, 22
    rabbit hair, 14, 22
    silk, 14, 22

vicuña, 14
wool, 13-14, 23-24, 27-28, 43
worsted, 43
yak hair, 14, 22
see also Yarns

B

Back apron, 121-22
Back beam, 110
Basket weave, 98-99
Bast fibers, 12
    hemp, 13
    jute, 13, 75
    linen, 12
Beaming the loom, 122-23
Beater, 110
Beating the weft, 83, 128
Bird's eye point twill, 101
Boat shuttle, 125

165

Bobbin tension screw, of a spinning wheel, 55
Bobbin winder, 125-26
Brake band, of a spinning wheel, 50
Breast beam, 110, 124
Broken twill, 101
Broken warp ends, repairing, 128
Butterfly hand bobbin, 80

C

Camel hair, 9, 14, 22
Carders, 28
Carding wool, 28-33
Cashmere, 14, 22
Chinese loom, 4
Cleaning skeins of wool, 57, 61
Cloth aprons, of a loom, 110
Cloth beam, 110
Cochineal, 60, 63
Combing wool, 26
Consignment selling, 156
Contre-marche looms, 108, 109
Cording, weaving with, 90
Corriedale sheep, 24
Cotton, 11, 22, 75
Counterbalanced looms, 109
Cow hair, 22
Craft's cooperatives, 156
Crimp, of wool, 23, 24
Cross of warp ends, 113

D

Dents, in reeds, 112
Designing your weaving, 105, 107-13
Designs to weave, 91-105
Direct tie-up, 98
Distaff, 21, 46
Dog hair, 22
Double driving band, of spinning wheel, 50
Dowel harness, 74
Drafts, of weaving patterns, 91-105
    overshot, 103
    rosepath, 101
    for tabby, 98-99
    for twill, 97-98
Draw-down, in draft of pattern, 93, 96
Driving band, of spinning wheel, 50
Dyeing, 59-69
    equipment, 61-62
    mordants, 60, 62-63
    safety in, 61
    top-dyeing, 60

    unspun fibers, 60
    woven fabric, 60
    yarns, 60
    see also Dyes
Dyes, 60
    animal, 59
    chemical, 59, 62
    natural, 59, 62-63
    plant, 64-69
    substantive, 60
    see also Plant dyes

E

E.p.i., 112

F

Ferns, dyeing with, 66
Fibers, 7-17
    animal, 7, 13-14, 22
    bast, 12, 74
    natural, 11-14
    plant, 7, 11-13
    seed fibers, 11
    synthetic, 7, 17
50/50 weave, 112
Flax, 21
Fleece, 24
    sorting, 24-26
Floor loom, 107-9
    see also Four-harness loom
Four-harness loom, 107-52
    parts, 109-10
    types, 107-9
    weaving on, 110-36
Frame loom, 71-74, 91
    buying, 74
    making, 74
    weaving on, 83-90
Fringing, 86
Front apron, 124

G

Ghiordes knot, 87-90
Goat hair, 14, 22
Goldenrod, dyeing with, 67-69
Grasses, weaving with, 90

H

Hand-chaining, 116
Harnesses, 5, 74, 110
Heading, 126

166

Heddles, 72, 93, 110, 120-21
Hemp, 13, 21
High wheel, 46
Human hair, 22

I

Indigo, 63
Interlocking weft, 140-41

J

Jack looms, 108
Jute, 13, 21, 75

K

Kilim tapestries, 137
Krokbragd weave, 149-52

L

Lag wool, 24
Lams, 94
Lanolin in wool, 24
Lazy Kate, 44
Lease sticks, 117
Leather bearing, of a spinning wheel, 55
Linen, 12, 21
Llama hair, 14
Loom, 2
  backstrap, 2
  beaming, 122-23
  Chinese, 4
  four-harness, 107-52
  frame, 71-74
  warp-weighted, 2
  waste, 111
Low wheel, 46, 49

M

Madder, 63
Marigold flowers, dyeing with, 65
Merino sheep, 24
Mohair, 14, 22
Mollusks, used in dyeing, 59
Mordants, 60, 61, 62-63
  alum, 60, 62
  chrome, 60, 62, 63

N

Napkins, making, 90
Natural fibers, 11-14

Niddy-noddy, 55
Nob, of spindle, 34
Noils, 26
Nonfibrous material, 7
Numbering system for identifying yarns,
  10, 24

O

Onion skins, dyeing with, 64-65
Overshot weave, 102

P

Patterns for weaving, 91-105
Pick (row), 4
Place mats, making, 90
Plain weave, 72
Planning your project, 105-13
Plant dyes,
  berries, 63
  coffee, 63
  ferns, 66
  fruits, 63
  goldenrod, 67-69
  leaves, 63
  marigold flowers, 65
  onion skins, 63, 64-65
  tea leaves, 63, 67
Plant fibers, 7, 11-13; in spinning, 21-22
  bast fibers, 12
  hemp, 13
  jute, 13, 75
  linen, 12
  cotton, 11, 21, 75
  flax, 21
  grasses, 90
  hemp, 13, 21
  jute, 13, 21
  linen, 12, 21
  raffia, 90
  seed fiber, 11
  sisal, 21
  see also Yarns
Plied yarns, 9
Plying yarns, 44, 55
Polyester, 17
Point twill, 101
Ponchos, making, 90
Projects to weave, 75-90, 132-34, 142-52

R

Rabbit hair, 14, 22
Raffia, 90

Rayon, 17
Reed, 110
Reed hook, 118
Return twill, 101
Rolags, 29, 43
Romeldale sheep, 24
Rosepath point twill, 101
Roving wool, 9
Rugs, making, 90
Ruler harness, 74
Rya technique, 87, 89

S

Satin weave, 97
Scarves, making, 90
Scouring wool, 57
Seed fiber, 11
Selling your work, 153-57
Sett, 112
Shaft, of spindle, 34
Shed, 4
Sheep, 24
Shuttles, 124-26
Silk, 14, 22
Singles yarn, 9
Sisal, 21
Skeining yarn, 55
Ski shuttle, 125
Skirtings, 24
Skirts, making, 89
Sleying, 112, 118-20
Slits, in a tapestry web, 137-39
Slivers, 9, 12
Slub yarn, 9
Snail's trail pattern, 103-5
Soumak techniques, 136
Spindle, 34-36
    nob, 34
    shaft, 34
    spinning with, 36-45
    whorl, 34
Spinning, 19-57
    choosing wool for, 24
    with a spindle, 36-45
    with a spinning wheel, 49-55
    twisting of yarn during, for strength, 9
    woolen, 23-24, 43
    worsted, 43
Spinning wheel, 46-55
    buying, 48
    spinning with, 49-55
    tension adjusting, 50-55
Staples, 24
String heddles, 74

S-twisted yarn, 44, 55
Synthetic fibers, 7, 17
    acrylic, 17
    polyester, 17
    rayon, 17
    see also Yarns

T

Tabby weave, 72, 87
    writing a draft for, 91-96, 98-99
Table looms, 107-8
Tapestry
    shuttle, 124-25
    weaving, 136-41
Tea leaves, dyeing with, 67
Teasing wool, 27-28
Tension screw, of a spinning wheel, 50, 55
Threading draft, 92
Throwing the shuttle, 128
Tie-up, in draft of pattern, 94
Top-dyeing, 60
Top wool, 24
Tops, 9, 26
Treadle, 46, 48, 50-52, 95, 110
Twill weave, 97, 100-103

U

Umbrella swift, 55

V

Vertical stripes, how to weave, 115
Vicuña, 14

W

Warp, 1, 8, 14, 124
    winding, 113-16
    warping the loom, 117
Warp beam, 110
Warp-faced weaving, 112
Warp reel, 55, 113
Warp-weighted loom, 2
Warping board, 113
Warpway stripes, how to weave, 115
Web, 1
Weft, 1, 8, 14, 83, 126
Weft-faced weaving, 112
Whorl, of spindle, 34
Wind-in sticks, 123
Wool, 13-14
    carding, 28-29
    combing, 26
    crimp, 23

fleece, 24
in the grease, 24
lag, 24
lanolin in, 24
numbering system, 10, 24
roving, 24
scouring, 57
skirtings, 24
sorting, 25-26
spinning with, 23-24
staples, 24
teasing, 27-28
top, 24
Woolen spinning, 43, 55
Worsted spinning, 43, 55

Y

Yak hair, 14, 22
Yarns, 7
    calculating amount needed, 112

choosing, 8, 14, 17
handspun vs. machine made, 21
numbering system, 10, 24
plied, 9
plying, 44
singles, 9
skeining, 55
slub, 9
strength, 8, 9
structure, 8-9
S-twisted, 44, 55
for warping, 8
for weft, 8
yarn count, 10
Z-twisted, 44, 55
see also Animal fibers, Plant fibers,
    Synthetic fibers

Z

Z-twisted yarn, 44, 55